May No Soldier Go Unloved
By Jeff Bader

"The greatest and highest level of giving is the person who gives without knowing for whom the gift is made, and the recipient does not know from whom he receives. And it matters not who makes the request for the gift or how it is made. The joyful and true giver cares not."
Maimonides

"Here's the challenge. Give an Ear. Heed the message. I warrant there's vinegar and pepper in it. Aye, the challenge ignites the heart."
William Shakespeare

"We make a living by what we get, but we make life of what we give."
Winston Churchill

"You make a decision. You determine what you should do with your life. How much are you willing to sacrifice? How much are you willing to give of yourself, your time, your love, your resources? You give. And you give until the Lord stops giving to you. When you do, you find life has taken on a whole new meaning."
John Lewis Russell

May No Soldier Go Unloved
by Jeff Bader
© 2007 by Angel Press Inc.
All rights reserved.

ISBN 978-0-6151-4690-4
LCCN

Printed in the United States of America.

Second Edition

May no soldier go unloved

May no soldier walk alone

May no soldier be forgotten,

Until they all come home.

Introduction

Patti Patton Bader has the heart of Mother Teresa, the motivational mastership of Vince Lombardi and the mobilization skills of Genghis Khan. She was raised an army brat; the great niece of the famous World War II General George S. Patton, daughter of decorated Vietnam Veteran Lt. Colonel David W. Patton, and sister of Iraqi War Veteran David Patton. When her oldest son Brandon was sent to Iraq during Operation Iraqi Freedom in the spring of 2003, she decided to send him at least one care package a day and keep a blog of the events that occurred in Iraq and

Afghanistan as an electronic scrapbook for Brandon when he returned. What started out as a mothers small commitment to her son has now turned into Soldiers Angels, an all volunteer organization with more than 100,000 members who aid and assist deployed soldiers all over the world. Soldiers Angels sends care packages and letters of encouragement to those in the field, provides first response backpacks and blankets of hope to the wounded, voice activated laptops to soldiers who have suffered hand, arm or sight injuries and "living trees" to the fallen hero's families who have paid the ultimate sacrifice. Patti has received numerous awards, accommodations, certificates and tons of letters of appreciation from soldiers, airmen, sailors, marines, family members, doctors, nurses, field commanders, sergeants, colonels, lieutenants, generals, the Surgeon General of the Army, the Secretary of Defense and the President of the United States (to name just a few). The Smithsonian Institute asked and was granted permission to host Patti's blog she started years ago, brandonblog.com which is still updated daily. Patti Patton Bader is a regular guest on numerous radio shows around the country and the stories of her and other Soldiers Angels deeds and ac-

Introduction

tions are published in local newspapers and magazines almost daily. Her newsletter alone raises several millions of dollars a year in donations. She takes not even one dime for compensation and does all of this from her bed with a laptop computer, a big screen TV and a cell phone. Patti has Hepatitis C and fibrosis of the liver and is often confined to her bed. She is in extreme pain most waking hours. I should know - I'm her husband. My wife is an amazing example of selflessness, patriotism, caring and dedication. Like an angel, she has anonymously and thanklessly touched the lives of many people she doesn't know. She works from the time she gets up in the early morning to the time she falls asleep from exhaustion late at night. Patti Patton Bader is a true American patriot. This is her story and the story of the founding of Soldiers Angels.

This book is dedicated to everyone who is or about to become a Soldiers Angel.

Special thanks to those bloggers who helped spread the message; Blackfive, Greyhawk, Lt. Smash, Sgt. Hook, Instapundit, Minstrelboy, Punditreview and many more. Keep your helmet on! Also thanks to our radio friends from coast to coast who helped us get the word out; Hugh Hewitt, Tara at Wolf Radio, Kevin and Bean, Laura Ingraham, G. Gordon Liddy, Ben Stein, Michelle Malkin and many many more. You're O.K. in my book!!!

We can't forget the great folks at Fund Raising Strategies who really made oceans of greatness possible. Thank you Bruce, Bob, and Matt.

And finally, a very special thanks to anyone who answered the call - and especially those who I've shamelessly omitted – you know who you are. Thank You. With all our heart, Patti and I love you.

Table of Contents

Patti Patton Bader at a Soldiers Angels booth
(Arcadia Park, Arcadia, CA Memorial Day 2005)

1

This Man Told Me...

My stepson Brandon crashed into the bedroom bursting with energy. "What honey?" Patti asked sleepily. She was in great pain from her Hepatitis C, still groggy from taking some pain pills, and was trying to sleep. "Mom, I'm going to join the Army!" Brandon grinned. "This man told me if I join the Army for three years I can be stationed in Italy, and they would pay for my college. I scored real high on their test."

Brandon, Patti's oldest son had graduated from high school that summer and was enrolled at San Diego State University. He was to start classes within the month and his mother and I were in the process of making the final arrangements (payment) for his dorm room. Brandon was a good student, but like most kids in college, he hadn't received a scholarship and was taking out student loans to pay for his education. He had calculated the total cost of tuition and books to be around $46,000 by the time he got his diploma. That price sounds inexpensive today, but at that time, it was a daunting amount of debt to incur when he would be just out of school. Brandon wanted to be independent and the Army was offering a lot of cool incentives including, of course, paying for college after his service. The incentives don't sound like much compared to those offered today, but at the time, seemed like a good idea as long as a big war didn't break out somewhere, God forbid.

Patti had taught Brandon about his military lineage. His Great Great Uncle was General George S. Patton, the famous World War II general. His grandfather was Lt. Colonel David W. Patton, West Point Class of 1955, and a decorated Vietnam Veteran who served two tours in the late 1960's. His Uncle David Patton was a specialist with the Mountain Rangers and had served in Afghanistan and later in Iraq. His mother Patti had moved from military base to military base as a child and had grown up in Fort Ord California, Fort Benning Georgia, Fort Campbell Kentucky, Fort Leavenworth Kansas, the American Embassy in Guatemala and the Patton Estate in San Marino, California. She taught her kids to have a sense of loyalty to family, patriotism and pride for their country and worship for God. Brandon helped around the house, saluted the flag, attended church on his own and sometimes volunteered his time for worthy causes; but I didn't think he had a strong call to service or a military sense of duty. His new decision was out of left field and for days I thought Brandon would change his mind. I played devils advocate and tried to make sure he had all the arguments presented to make a sound decision. His mother and I paid for his dorm room so he wouldn't feel cornered into this new life altering plan and he still had some of his options open.

One week before September 11, 2001, Brandon signed the papers and officially joined the Army as a Private. None of us knew it at the time, but Brandon had just rolled a little snowball off a big snowy mountain which would very shortly become a giant avalanche of love and support called Soldiers Angels.

2

Go You Brits!

Brandon had joined the Army 4th Infantry and his three years of service stationed in Italy had suddenly turned into 4 years at Fort Sills in Oklahoma. Most military recruiters are super salesmen. Brandon was going to be an artillery specialist, and would be learning the Army's new computerized weapons systems like those that were used in the M109 Paladin artillery launchers.

A Paladin is the most technical artillery weapon that the Army has in its arsenal and looks like a tank with a giant howitzer cannon sticking out of it. Brandon was the quickest video game player I had ever seen, and coincidently, the Army's newly computerized weapons systems are almost identical in nature and use those exact same computer skills.

Go You Brits!

Patti made sure that everyone in the family wrote Brandon a cheerful letter from home and I remember mailing a really funny one on September 10. The next morning I greatly regretted sending it. Brandon later told us that a C.O. (Commanding Officer) rushed into his barracks on the morning of September 11 and announced "AMERICA HAS BEEN ATTACKED HUNDREDS OF THOUSANDS OF AMERICANS HAVE BEEN KILLED WE ARE GOING TO WAR WE ARE ACCELERATING YOUR TRAINING YOU WILL BE ON THE BATTLEFIELD WITHIN THE MONTH GET READY HOO-AH!" During boot camp in the Army, soldiers have no access to T.V, radio, or a newspaper and I imagined how scared those recruits had to be that day. Most of them were just kids.

It wasn't until March of 2003 that Brandon and the 4th Infantry would be sent to Iraq. During the preceding year, Patti passionately watched the news and when the American press and U.S. Government started censoring the news reports coming out of the Middle East, Patti started subscribing to all the other world news services. The day Brandon set foot in Kuwait, Patti started a daily blog called brandonblog.com, that recorded the news events of the day that impacted our deployed soldiers in Iraq from *all* of the world news services.

As Brandon entered Iraq in the spring of 2003, Patti started catnapping in the hours that news wasn't coming out of Iraq, and coordinated her waking hours for the prime time reports that would be broadcast on live T.V. from the newly embedded news reporters. Baghdad is almost 12 hours difference from our time in Pasadena, California. I would awake to the sound of Patti cheering on our soldiers at 3 and 4 A.M. in the morning. On one of the first nights of the Iraq War she swelled up with so much emotion that she screamed at the T.V. "Go You Brits!!!" as the British troops stormed Basra, Iraq. Not knowing what was going on, I jumped out of bed and raced out into the living room with a baseball bat to confront the intruders. I got used to her nightly exuberance after that. I also discovered Patti had been a cheer-leader in high school.

As Brandon's unit entered Iraq we started to keep all of our TV's on 24/7 to all the different cable news stations for updates.

Go You Brits!

One day within the first month that Brandon's unit was in Iraq I was sure I saw him for just a nanosecond on Fox news during a night time raid on a compound in Tikrit. Although we knew his unit was based around Al Fallujah at the time, we were sure it was him. Patti and I called all of our relatives and made them promise to watch the repeat broadcast later that evening. Every one of us agreed it was most certainly Brandon (although he had lost a lot of weight) and I even ordered a special tape of the broadcast for posterity. It's funny how all of us were blinded by the overwhelming desire to connect with a loved one at war, even for a millisecond. A year later, when Brandon returned, we showed the tape to him to everyone's hearty laughter. We weren't even close.

After the first month of the war in Iraq, Patti started settling into a new routine: she would Brandonblog from 5 AM until noon, take a small nap and then rise for the evening newscasts at 5 PM, then wait for the live reporting from Baghdad that usually started around 11 PM and lasted until early in the morning. Pretty soon her blog was ranking as high as the major news networks in Google and the other web search engines when some-one was "surfing" for the news from Iraq. Even today, if you type in the search term "Iraq or Iraqi War News" or similar search words in the major web search engines like Google, MSN, Yahoo, etc., brandonblog.com will rank with or above CBS, MSNBC, ABC, CNN, FOX, BBC, Reuters and even the UPI and the AP websites.

In early 2005 the Smithsonian Institute contacted Patti and requested to host brandonblog.com as an educational resource about the War in Iraq. Today brandonblog.com (iraqwarnews.net) is one of the largest collections of information, news articles and pictures about Operation Iraqi Freedom and it is updated daily by a volunteer Angel.

3

The Luckiest Man In Iraq

Dear Brandon,

It is Saturday before Easter. Jeff is reading the paper and I am watching the news freaking out. They won't give us much info so I don't know where you are. I imagine you are camping out most nights so God bless you son because I know it's very uncomfortable. I hope your packages come soon. Please write and let me know what you need. I love you brave one.

Love,

Mom

May No Soldier Go Unloved

Patti had consulted her father on what she could do to help

Brandon while he was deployed and the Lt. Colonel (Ret.) told

her to send care packages in shoeboxes. "Anything larger takes a

lot longer to arrive." Patti and I became experts in over-packing

and sending our shoebox care packages to Brandon. We checked

the military website and learned the do's and don'ts of sending

care packages to APO (Army Post Office) addresses overseas.

Patti and I went shopping and bought the miniature toiletries and

lots of beef jerky, gum, candy and cans of Brandon's favorite

raviolis. We learned that he needed sand scarves to keep the

sand out of his eyes during the fierce Iraqi sandstorms, baby

wipes to keep his gun clean and powdered Gatorade to give the

water some flavor and keep his electrolyte count up. It is either

really cold in Iraq or really hot, and when it's hot, in order not to

get dehydrated, each soldier needs to drink *an extra* eight quarts

of water or more daily. The Lt. Colonel (Ret.) told us it takes a

minimum of 2 to 4 weeks for an APO package to arrive in Iraq.

Patti sent Brandon packages 2 weeks before he even arrived in

Kuwait. The first day we could, we sent 10 packages and continued sending two and three packages daily to Brandon's APO address.

About a month and a half after his deployment we still had no word on Brandon or his unit other then to know they were in a city called Al Fallujah. Patti couldn't stand it anymore and searched the Fort Sill website for a way to gather more information. She found a Red Cross phone number and they referred her to the Rear Detachment Support Group who referred her to The Family Readiness Group (FRG) who referred her to Rosana R. - Brandon's' Sergeants wife stationed at Fort Sill, Oklahoma. Patti introduced herself and asked about Brandon and his Unit. "I haven't heard about your son, I'll ask my husband about Brandon next time I hear from him. Call me back in a couple days. I know they are out there in the middle of it, carrying guns, sleeping in the desert, things are bad for them." Patti and I doubled our outgoing packages.

When Patti called Rosana the next week she had some news. "I asked my husband about your son, and he said, who Brandon? You mean the luckiest man in Iraq?" YES!!! Brandon was getting our packages and was okay! We weren't going to be able to afford the new house Patti wanted, but we didn't care. Sending a loved one to war is a life-altering experience for everyone involved. It puts life's problems into a totally different perspective. We stopped sweating about the small stuff.

Word was getting out among Brandon's Unit and pretty soon other parents, husbands and wives were calling and asking Patti's advice on how to get their packages to their deployed loved ones faster and more efficiently. Finally Brandon got a chance to call home. "Brandon, are you getting your packages?" she asked. "Yes Mom, can you send more?" We were flabbergasted. We had sent Brandon over 100 packages in two months. "Most guys here are getting very little from home and some guys are getting nothing." He explained. "I share my packages with them." Patti the mom immediately asked for the names and APO addresses of those who weren't receiving anything and as soon as she got off the phone with Brandon, immediately started calling all our friends and relatives. Soon Patti was "adopting" out soldiers in Brandon's unit to everyone we knew.

The Luckiest Man In Iraq

The 4th Infantry were the first U.S. soldiers in Iraq to enter Al Fallujah, Ar Ramadi, the Al Asad Air Force Base, and secure the Syrian border during Operation Iraqi Freedom. They slept in tents with giant camel spiders and ate only military MRE's (Meals-Ready-to-Eat) for the first few months.

Besides the snacks and hygiene items, Patti and I also shipped laptop computers, portable DVD players and later, even air conditioners to Iraq. Patti wanted her son and his buddies to come home safe and sane; and for Christmas that year Patti and I bought each member in Brandon's entire battery a small Christmas package filled with a phone card, hot chocolate, a snack and a few other small items.

Patti was gaining a reputation for her generosity and Brandon was gaining a reputation as a team player and stand-up guy. I was going broke. That fall Brandon was promoted to Corporal in the field and received 14 accommodations during his tour in Iraq. Patti's plan on supporting Brandon was working well, now she had her sites fixed on helping the other hundred thousand deployed servicemen and women.

May No Soldier Go Unloved

22 July 2003

Headquarters
2nd Battalion, 5th Field Artillery
Paladin Base
Ar Ramadi, Iraq

Hello everyone,

It has been a month since I arrived at Paladin Base and nearly a month since I assumed command of this great battalion. As you know I have worked very hard to improve information flow in the battalion to try to keep you as informed as possible about what your husbands are doing and how they are living. We will continue to send out regular updates. I will also send out a letter like this on a monthly basis to provide you information straight from me. I will make a point to include as much information, good and bad, as possible, with the exception of details I must omit for operational security reasons. Rest assured that the soldiers are performing well and gaining quite a reputation for their professionalism. You should all be proud of them and the job they are doing. We continue to make improvements in the battalion daily. The little things count like maintenance of

The Luckiest Man In Iraq

vehicles, soldier discipline, and taking care of the soldiers in terms of quality of life initiatives that the previous chain of command started and we are going to push. In line with that, my priorities are pretty simple: mission accomplishment, maintenance and taking care of soldiers. With that, of course, is a condition of maintaining a proactive force protection posture and safe operation is stressed from start to finish in all that we do. You really see the difference when you see our soldiers around soldiers from other units. Our guys always have their helmets and flak jackets on, clean weapons and are very much aware of where they are and what they are doing. I am confident that our soldiers and leaders are prepared. Most of the Iraqis that we deal with are decent people just trying to make a living. That is to say that there is no danger where we are operating. There are still those with ill intent and we work on them as well, to date we've delivered several to the detention facility to keep them out of circulation. We are pretty scientific about what we do, where we go, and how we do things. We rehearse extensively and stay within our capabilities. While everyone else is looking for Saddam and the guys who made the famous playing cards, we focus on local terrorists that threaten a safe a secure environment in our area of operations. Put them in jail before they can do any harm is the philosophy. The alternative is allowing the local thug to pick the time and the place. Redeployment rumors have been rampant since I arrived here at the Battalion. When the battalion left Fort Sill the orders said from 6 months to a year. Since 2-5 FA is in direct support of the 3rd Armored Cavalry Regiment, our redeployment is tied to their mission accomplishment. If you have been following the news, like I do, you will know there is an anticipated requirement for troops to remain up to a year. What that means for us is that we expect to stay until Mar/Apr 04. That may not be what you want to hear, but I believe that saying nothing is worse than dealing with the stress of the unknown. Please feel free to pass on any feedback or questions you may have about these letters to Kristi (head of the Rear Detachment Group)*, or have your husbands speak with the chain of command. I'll do my best to answer your questions and keep you*

16

informed. Thanks again for everything. See you on the flight line.

Sincerely,

David. H. LTC, FA Commanding

Dear Ms. Patton,

I am SPC. Chad T, your son's gunner. I would like to tell you how grateful we are that your son has decided to serve his country by serving in the U.S. Army. Furthermore, we would like to thank you for intrusting your son to the Army's care. I would like to tell you how proud I am to have Brandon as a member of my sector. He is an excellent soldier and a great example for the other members of the section to follow. He is by far one of the hardest working soldiers in the Battery. Finally, I would like to thank your family a very Merry Christmas and a Happy New Year from all the soldiers and NCO's of Bravo Battery 2nd BN 5th FA.

Sincerely,

SPC Chad T.

May No Soldier Go Unloved

Mrs. Patton,

Hello, my name is Sgt. Michael D. I am in you sons unit. I wanted to write you and thank you for everything that you are doing for the soldiers of this unit. It is greatly appreciated. You have played a big impact on the morale and motivation of these soldiers. Even though we do not know you personally we all hold a special spot in our heart for you. Your son is doing a great job out here. You really couldn't ask for anymore from a soldier. He is always putting in the extra effort to accomplish the missions that he is given. He is an outstanding soldier, and a great person, which reflects on his upbringing. Everyone is pretty much safe here. There is no date of return. I expect to be here for the long haul. But we will make it. It's pretty hot now, but it's bearable. Once again, thanks for everything you've done.

Sincerely,

Sgt. Michael D. B2/5 FA BN

The Luckiest Man In Iraq

Dear Patti Patton-Bader,

Thank you very much for your kind note and box of goodies. It means a lot for me to hear from the families of the great soldiers in this battalion. Brandon is doing a great job in Bravo Btry and you should be proud of him for his service to this unit and the Country. My goals are to accomplish our mission and to bring all the soldiers home as quickly as I can. Right now that looks like April 2004. I know you are anxious to see Brandon home safely as I am.

Sincerely,

David H. LTC, FA.

I Know What I Want for Christmas

For the next several weeks Patti Patton Bader called all of our

relatives and friends and convinced them to help send more

packages to Brandon's Unit. She put up a "Wall of Honor" link

on her blog and listed the name of anybody who helped contrib-

ute. The first hundred or so of those listed on brandonblog.com

represent all of our relatives and friends that Patti could reach. It

wasn't long, however, until Patti started running out of friends

and relatives. That wasn't going to stop her. She just became

more proactive, and in September 2003 Patti Patton Bader put a

message board on her blog asking the American People for help.

She joined the Military Support Groups and linked with her fel-

low military bloggers. She called radio stations and pleaded that she be put on the air. She's a great interview and quite a motivator; and who didn't want to hear "Patton's" opinion about the war?

Within a few days, donations started rolling in and lots of people were asking to help. Other Americans who found out what Patti was doing also wanted to "adopt" soldiers and send them care packages and letters of encouragement. We were becoming a fulltime operation. We screened prospective "adopters" through my company, Accurate Credit Bureau, with a simple background check and if they were ok, Patti would give them the APO address of a deployed soldier from our son's battalion. Patti asked adopters to send a letter a week and a care package a month. She started calling adopters "Soldiers Angels," and Patti and I designed a website called soldiersangels.com which allowed soldiers to submit their names and APO addresses and in turn, Americans could adopt deployed soldiers and become "Soldiers Angels".

This concept of adopting a soldier directly with no "in between" organization was new and quite a success. Americans

could donate to Soldiers Angels or "adopt a soldier" and donate
directly to their adoptee and were personally responsible for
their care and well being, one-on-one, mano y mano. Naturally,
the biggest thrill for an Angel was to receive a letter or email
back from their adoptee. Without mentioning any names, some
of these letters have been known to make grown men cry. I
promise you, if you ever have the good fortune to receive one of
these letters; it will change your life forever (and put your worries in a whole different perspective).

Soldiers Angels was rapidly getting bigger and Patti started
enlisting help and delegating jobs to some of the other "Angels"
who made the mistake of calling her more then once. Patti personally called every adopting Angel who applied and told them
they were now an ambassador of Soldiers Angels and if they
heard or saw of any soldier or military family in need, it was
their duty to contact her immediately. She closed every new
Angel adopting conversation with "Welcome Angel" and said it
so often, because so many American's were adopting soldiers
that Brett and Bayley, Patti's other two kids still living at home,

started to lovingly mimic her, "Welcome Angel, Welcome Angel." She was too busy to hear us. Our phones started smoking at all hours of the day and night. Our mailbox was crammed with donations and letters. Accurate Credit Bureau turned into a shipping and receiving office for Soldiers Angels and A.C.B. employees volunteered their time to help pack the donated goods. All of the Post Office employees knew us by our first names. Friends were bribed and favors were called in. Patti is a whirlwind of energy.

She would arise at 4 AM and start working and wouldn't stop until midnight or later when she finally would fall asleep from exhaustion. I was beginning to worry about her health but her new "job" seemed to give her purpose and the results were exhilarating. For a woman in constant pain and pretty much confined to her bed, what Patti was accomplishing by internet and phone was nothing short of miraculous.

We started receiving letters of thanks and accommodations from Sergeants and Field Commanders telling us the Angel's support was helping the morale of the soldiers and making their life a lot better.

Around Thanksgiving my wife snuggled up to me, nibbled on my ear, and cooed "I know what I want for Christmas." She knows how to get what she wants. "I want a non-profit corporation so that the donations we receive can be tax deductible." It wasn't quite what I expected. A non-profit organization didn't sound very sexy.

We filed for the corporation in December 2003 and Soldiers Angels officially became a 501c 3 non-profit-corporation in March 2004; about the time our son, Corporal Brandon Varn, returned safely home from Iraq. Our website went from a .com to an .org. and Soldiers Angels was officially born. We even had our non-profit-corporation Tax ID. This was only the beginning.

Letters From Soldiers

Dear Mrs. Patti-Patton Bader,

Per our conversation will you please send to me the name of a medic. You are doing such a wonderful job. I am a Veteran of WW II and Korea.

Thank You,

Dean T. San Dimas, CA.

Dear Mrs. Patton-Bader,

Enclosed please find a check in the amount of $37.00 (thirty-seven dollars) for the purchase of three throw rugs and two pairs of sweat pants to be sent to soldier(s) at the Landstuhl Regional Medical Center. I served as a special tech in the 76th Field Hospital in the battle of Okinawa in 1944 and remember well the severe loneliness and distress our brave wounded men endured. Thank you for your fine efforts to provide some comfort and to support morale of our current brave soldiers.

Respectively,

Wilbert C. F. Lansing, MI

May No Soldier Go Unloved

To My Dear Soldier,

Hello, although we don't know each other, I am hoping this little letter will bring you a tie that binds and touches. Everyday my family and I watch the news and I think of you and remember you and your family in our prayers. I think you have remarkable strength and courage and you lift my heart with the sacrifices you have made and help me be strong. This letter and package are just a little something from home to let you know you are loved and thought of 24 – 7.

God bless you dear one,

From Eugene, Oregon. Tom, Chris, and Nancy

Letters From Soldiers

Dear Patti,

Your package arrived today at the perfect time. Supplies are a bit scarce due to the current operation and I've shared the lot with the soldiers I work with. Whatever is left over tomorrow will go forward to the guys out filling our battle positions. Thank you so much for being our Angel. It's warming to know that folks are thinking of us back home. Feel free to write anytime and I'll do my best to answer promptly though time is something we don't always have a lot of. Thank you again and take care.

Sincerely,

Kirk K. HHC/4-31 IN BN10th MTN DIV

Dear Patti Patton Bader,

Thank you so much. Your organization is wonderful and so help-ful. Please forward this message to all angels as I have received so many letters and packages from all over the world. I could not possible answer all of the angels due to time constraints in the war zone. Please tell everyone thanks so much, your letters and packages has saved me from going crazy some times. Any-

time someone gets mail here everybody perks up. I am assigned to the **** **** in **** Iraq as the night time helicopter pad Superintendent. This is a trauma hospital which receives patients such as: American, Iraqi civilians, Iraqi Police, Iraqi children and other allied NATO forces working with us. This hospital is in the Red Zone which is a bad place to be and gets mortared almost every day. So as you can see, any mail is greatly appreciated and we all share our gifts with each other. Keep up the great work.

MSgt Ronald

Hello All,

I am from Hampton Bays and serving as a Combat Medic in the Army in Baghdad. I am always searching for news from the home front. I am very moved by the support from home. Some things that are needed over here are....AA Batteries (for our hand-held radios), sometimes there is a huge shortage and communication isn't as easy without our Motorola radios. Also

Letters From Soldiers

Ramen Noodles are a delicacy (or any quick meal). We always enjoy encouraging letters...they are very touching! Drink mixes that we can pour in our bottled water is always a treat. American Flag stickers (believe it or not are hard to get a hold of here). Some of the soldiers here in my Company could probably use a pen-pal. Words of Support are mightier than any sword!
SGT. Shaun M.

Dear Ms. Patton-Bader,

Thank you for all your emails, letters, and packages. You all are wonderful and I am glad that I have the chance to communicate with such wonderful individuals. Take care and God Bless.
SSG McCoy

Mrs. Bader,

I have to tell you I have heard from a number of Angels already and they are all awesome. What a wonderful country we live in. You truly make our sacrifices worthwhile.
CPT T.

May No Soldier Go Unloved

Patti,

We do our duty because we said "I will" and you are making it a bit easier to spend the long days here away from family. Thank you for standing on point with us at the home front.

SGT S.

Dear Soldiers Angels,

My name is SPC Daniel B and I was told about your website through a friend. I am currently serving our great nation in Iraq with my unit HHC, 86th Signal Battalion. I have been away from my family for two and a half months and miss them more and more. I am proud to serve our nation in it's darkest hour. The morale of my soldiers is always on my mind. I can't begin to tell you how deep it weighs on my heart and mind that all our soldiers are dying for the freedoms we enjoy. I serve proud and realize it is for the better of our life, the American way of life. I am familiar with the work you guys are doing and it brings me joy to know Americans like you are supporting soldiers. We have a long ten months left in our deployment and we are asking for

31

any support. I have one soldier who could use a pair of running shoes. His feet are wide and the local PX doesn't carry the shoe necessary to accommodate his feet. He is a size ten. He loves new balance and Nike but will take anything. In Baghdad it is not easy to get good products. We appreciate any care packages and all the love shown from Soldiers Angels. I am sure you are well aware that a package can make a soldiers year, not just make his day. As the fight goes on the death toll continues to rise. We are ready and determined to fight the war on terrorism. Our families support us the best way they can. Some younger soldiers at war with wives and children back home find it harder to manage than others.

Again God Bless your efforts, God Bless all you do, God Bless America. The soldier is a size ten in the running shoe. If at all possible, I realize you guys can't help everybody. We are thankful for all you do for our soldiers. We promise to work hard for you, and stay focused on our mission.

SPC Daniel B. HHC, 86th Signal Battalion

May No Soldier Go Unloved

Dear Patti,

My name is Sgt Michael D and I am currently serving our great nation in Iraq. I submitted my information in hopes that a Soldier's Angel would respond. I have to say that I am the luckiest soldier here because I did link up with someone from you team. Her name is Stephanie L. from Connecticut. She is absolutely awesome and her dedication is overwhelming. I have found a new friend thanks to the Soldier's Angels organization. I couldn't be happier with my sponsor. I felt it important to notify someone of her outstanding support. Thank you!

Sgt Michael D. HHD 382nd MP BN

Patti,

Thank you so much for your support of the soldiers here in Afghanistan. My Unit, 5-7 ADA, just arrived here in Bagram and we will be here for one year. The weather here is starting to really get hot. The rainy season should be finished and next will be the dry, windy, and dusty season. I am originally from Kansas then I went to collage in Minnesota. I was then stationed in

Hanau, Germany before I was deployed. As for the package, I

am ensuring that the soldiers get all that is sent. I have some

soldiers at a remote base that need the items more then I do. So,

I am putting the box on a helicopter for those guys. Again, thank

you for all your support from back home.

Sincerely,

Sonya B. CJTF-76/5-7 ADA

Dear Patti Bader,

Thank you so much for your service to us. You probably don't

realize how much you brighten someone's face and day with a

simple letter or a small package. I have given your address to

my whole platoon! Some don't have a strong family support

group. Moms and Dads sometimes just don't understand. I hope

they all contact you. When my Soldier received the envelope that

you sent out, I heard her squeal!! So thank you, thank you, thank

you. God Bless,

SFC Bridget C. HHC 4th BOTB 4th BCT 506th RCT 101st ABN

May No Soldier Go Unloved

Dear Patti Bader,

I don't know how to begin to thank you. I was so surprised to see you had sent two boxes of the shampoo and conditioner...and not just any kind, but the "good stuff." I gave it out to the females in my platoon, then to the females in another platoon that I work with, and I still had 4 bottles left. I gave them to the females in other sections who have helped me out a lot. All the females were impressed with the Biolage. One PFC even said "Yes! I love this stuff but I left mine at home!" I want you to know how much we all appreciated your gift. A couple of the girls asked for your address as well. Thank you so much again. You'll never really know how much support means. Have a Happy Thanksgiving and a great holiday season. (Also thank you for supporting Soldiers Angels. It's a great organization and does so much for us.)

Respectively,

Lisa S. 1 LT, OD Platoon Leader

Letters From Soldiers

Dear "Army Mom,"

Just wanted to take a second to tell you what happened in Iraq today. It was raining - and I was just coming in to my headquarters when I passed by one of my newer soldiers - an immigrant from the former Soviet Union - and one of my BEST privates. I was stopped in my tracks, for behold - on such a dreary day he was smiling. I was being funny (at first) and I said "awww you got a package with some goodies? Who sent that to you?" And as I expected to hear him say "my mom (or something like that)" he turned his face to me and said "I don't know...." he had a smile on his face.....and as I saw his eyes glazing he said "...that's why I was smiling" and at that my eyes began to glaze too. I can never take for granted their service, not for one minute - not for one second. And now...even in a hell hole like this - God has sent yet another Angel. I'll bet you didn't know that did you? How truly amazing - how close we come to God in such a far away place. And how silly I am for thinking that this private's safety is for me only to keep. Seems there are many who share this burden-and make me sleep sound. You made one of my sol-

diers smile today - sitting there by himself - and for that, you

have touched my soul. I'd thank you, but that's not why Angels

do what they do (I know). So instead I'll just say - Well Done!

You can rest easy, message received. And I'll do my best to bring

them home. I Owe God one ;-) Thank you from my soul,

Sergeant Steve S.

PS From the Fourth Army son of a mom like you no doubt.

Dear Patti,

Thank you for your superb organization. We truly appreciate the

support. We will be sure to update on any changes to informa-

tion. We could use some mach 3 razors, razor refills, and

disposable razors. Also, we need liquid body wash, shampoo,

tuna lunch packs, beef jerky, hard candy, Capri sun drinks, lots

of tan army shirts, green or black calf socks, or anything else

you might think we need. And thanks for sending your letter to

check on me. Pro Patria,

Nick and Guys

Letters From Soldiers

Dear Ms. Bader,

I wanted to thank you for the coffee and grinder. My name is SPC Donna S. I am a medic assigned with the 28th Combat Support Hospital in Baghdad, Iraq. One of the sergeants that works for me is a true coffee hound. He is hoarding the grinder. None of us are allowed to touch it or make coffee. I appreciate you thinking of us. It helps to know that people back home aren't believing everything they see on the news. Please continue to think of us. Sincerely,

Donna R. S. SFC USA NCO1C Department of Pharmacy

Dear Patti,

Thank you so much for your wonderful and thoughtful donations. I received the backpacks today and I am thrilled. I am an ICU nurse at the hospital in Baghdad and know everything will be put to good use. We see many different types of patients from U.S. to coalition to Iraqi from life threatening injuries to bumps and bruises. We even see many children. As a nurse the hardest patient to have is the wounded American Soldier. They are all such wonderful men and women and it is very difficult to see

these injuries. The backpacks offer some of the comforts of home

I know they appreciate. In the ICU these soldiers are very sick

and are usually unable to use many things but when we get them

ready to transport we wrap them in one of your blankets. We

hope this blanket makes it all the way back to the states. For

some of the less injured patients they are able to wear the

sweatpants and use the shower kits. Thank you again so much.

Soldiers Angels is a wonderful organization which is making a

difference in all of our lives here.

Thank you again,

CPT Ann B. U.S. Army Nurse 28th CSH

Letters From Soldiers

Soldiers Angels,

I just wanted to write you a quick note of thanks for the wonderful backpacks you sent the 28th CSH. The items were used by both injured soldiers and soldiers stationed at the hospital. It is heartwarming to know how many Americans are thinking about us while we are deployed and defending our freedoms. God bless all of you.

Sincerely,

CPT Kara W. Physical Therapist ACO TFN 28th CSH

Patti,

*First of all let me take the time to **thank you**. Your support of our young Airman, Soldiers, Sailors and Marines is greatly appreciated. Knowing that we have your support back home means more then anything you can provide. However, let me also thank you for the care package. I've shared your Care Package with some of my younger troops and hopefully they will find time to keep in touch with a letter or thank you card. The conditions here are not that austere. But it's a wonderful feeling when you* *receive any type of correspondence from the states. Many of these brave soldiers and marines are on the front lines securing America from future terrorist attacks. Many of them do not have the luxery of a hot meal, hot shower, or clean shave in weeks. Once a week we gather in a large building called the morale center. This is where we share our care packages, books, magazines and of course lettes with our front line soldiers. Anything left over is donated to the resident chaplain for distributed down range. The duty for us is actually not bad. The DoD has made significant improvements since the first Gulf War. The government invested a lot of money into a company named Kellog, Brown, and Root. They are contracted to keep the facilities clean, provide laundry service and serve pre-cooked meals. It's not a hotel, but it's not horribly bad either. Due to the extreme nature of the job we are limited on "fun" stuff here. Most spend off-duty time in the make-shift gym, reading or watching DVD movies that are donated from the states. Personally, I enjoy watching CNN and keeping up-to-date with America and sports; especially the New York Yankees! My group arrived in early*

Letters From Soldiers

February and is scheduled to leave in early June. Most of us who arrived in January will be home by July. There is a small group who will be here an additional 2-3 weeks for turnover. Myself, I'll be returning home to my Air Force base in Tokyo Japan. Most likely I'll remain there until September 2007 then hopefully move/retire to Washington State. Yes, we are trying to stay on an area with a rich Japanese culture. My wife is Japanese and is currently working as a nurse assistant in a retirement home and attending college. She is hoping t one day become a certified nurse. Me, well I've been in the Air Force for 27 years. Hopefully I can stay in till 30 then retire. After that, who knows? I'll probably stay with the Armed Forces in some capacity of government service. I love my country, it's way of life and the men and women who bravely serve her each and every day. Right now we are starting to get hot weather. Yesterday was 98+ degrees in the shade and tomorrow will reach 100. It's actually not bad, just makes you tired more then anything else. Time is going by pretty quickly. We don't talk about the "bad" stuff happening in Iraq. We each deal with it in our own

May No Soldier Go Unloved

*way, attend mass and pray. I can't wait to see the mountains, trees, and flowers once again. As much as I hate traffic and big cities, that won't be such a bad site to see either. After 5 months this tour is finally almost over. In about 3 weeks I'll start to pack, catch a military flight and start a long 56 hour journey back home. Even thou I'm no youngster, my Mom still worries about me each and everyday. And it will be a great feeling to call her and say I'm home. Once again, **thank you**....it means so much to know America cares. These brave freedom fighters are doing everything possible to defend and preserve your way of life. Please continue to support your troops. It's patriots like you that make each day a little easier. God Bless America and have a safe and happy Memorial Day from the Mean and Women of the Combined Task Force – Arabian Peninsula Iraq.*

Sincerely,

Bradley

Letters From Soldiers

Dear Soldiers Angels,

I just wanted to take a minute to say thank you for your support. The Soldiers Angels program really let people know out there who appreciate what we are doing out here. I think what means the most is not that any of the letters focused on the War itself but the soldiers like myself who are away from our families for a year or more. Knowing so many people are praying for our safety means a lot and all the letters I received really meant a lot.

Just wanted to say thanks,

SPC. Maurice A. C. 418 Medlog

Dear Patti,

I received your box tonight and I wanted to Thank You Dearly. Myself and my soldiers greatly appreciate your support and kindness. The thermal undergarment were especially needed and I love the t-shirts. I gave the thermals to the needy soldiers and myself and the Commander will sport the T-Shirts. It's great and heart warming to know that you guys really care and support us in these trying times. The weather has really gotten cold. We've moved to a new location, so we haven't gotten any heating sources yet. It's about 11 pm right now and I've got soldiers out checking for bad guys on the streets and in neighborhoods. Every night they go out I just pray that they all arrived back safely. So far, we've been fortunate....Thank God! Even though we spend Thanksgiving here, we got a pretty decent meal. Christmas is around the corner and I can see the frustration in everyones eyes. However we will continue to push and hope that the days will pass by, so that we can all go home some day. Wee, enough of that. So, how's the weather in Pasadena and how are you? Hope all is doing well. I can only wish the best for you and know that your contributions to us will not be unnoticed.. God Bless and warm Holiday Greetings to you.

Sincerely,

Ricky

Letters From Soldiers

To all that donated,

Thank you for your donations to American Soldiers. I am very grateful and so are the four platoons who benefited from your donation of coffee and snacks. The best thing about your gift was not the coffee and snacks but the notes of support. I have shared those with my whole unit, it lets us know we are receiving your prayers! This has been a blessing.

Thank you again,

Lt Lynae De G. "Nurse"

Dear Friends,

I write this from my deployed location in support of the global war on terror from Southwest Asia. First, I want to say that I am incredibly thankful for the overwhelming response and support that is being funneled though me to the airman, soldiers, sailors, and even an occasional marine who serves with me here in my location. I'm not at liberty to give many details about our operation here, but I can share that what is being done here is nothing short of amazing. Let me tell you about some of the folks you have reached out and touched. Some of you sent school supplies, blankets, and other items for local children and adults. Our base has many neighbors, many of whom have tarps as roofs over their heads. But the location has a real heart beat and is coming alive to the sound of freedom. Schools are beginning to open, and in many cases are able to do so because of the generous do-nations of supplies from the states. It is warm here most of the time, but in the winter can get quite cold, especially at night. Blankets can make a life or death difference. Others of you have sent items to show your support for our military members de-ployed along side of me. Many of them have some difficult and demanding jobs. Some stand exposed guarding our perimeters. I cannot brag enough on our medical folks who I have seen save the life and limbs of many people. Our engineers are doing amazing things to bring improvements to our facilities. We have army troops who risk their lives patrolling neighborhoods and keeping the peace. Sometimes they are on the receiving end of attacks. And yes they have lost brothers in arms. Some of them have returned wounded. Sometimes the insurgents strike at our base itself. We are not shaken. We stand strong in the freedom

that we enjoy as a nation. Many of these troops join me weekly

for worship and Bible studies. These are the most dynamic peo-

ple of great character I have ever had the privilege to work with.

They are nothing short of amazing. In my time here I've had the

opportunities to minister to these troops out with them standing

post on the wire, carrying wounded to the medical facility, and

even carrying the dead on their first steps home. I've stood in

formation with my brothers and sisters and rendered farewell

tributes to the dead were gently placed on aircraft to come

home. I've rejoiced and celebrated news of births and other

moments of joy. I've cried with a father whose wife miscarried.

I've comforted the sick and honored the dead. I've lead worship

and been lead in worship. I have counseled over a wide range of

issues. I've taught and I've learned. I have been a friend and

been befriended. In all things I have seen the power of God at

work in His people here. I truly thank you for you support you

have provided through Operation Outreach whether you do-

nated to Operation Aircare in support of our troops of

May No Soldier Go Unloved

Operation School Supplies helping us win the hearts and minds of people by showing the true heart of Americans. Thank you for helping me care for our people. I've had the opportunity to do so many things here that I am thankful for having had the privilege. One of the most proud is being able to reach back and give something to these fine men and women who are serving their country and to reach out to a people struggling to create a prosperous nation. It really is about people and you have helped me make the difference, and for that I thank you.

Sincerely,

David D. R. Chaplain, Captain USAF 506 AEG STAFF/EHC

Letters From Soldiers

Ana – Marie Smith, Patti Bader, and Soldiers Angels,

My name is 2nd Lt. Jimmy L. I just wanted to say thank you to all of you there. I had never heard of your organization but my grandmother has been contributing to you for a while now I guess. I wasn't sure what to expect when she said I would be getting a care package from you but I assure you that when it arrived I along with my Marines were grateful and found a good use or need for all the items. The beverage packs were a big hit along with the meal and snack packs. Once again I would like to say thank you and your organization. It really helps boost the morale of a lot of the younger Marines who feel like a lot of those back home have forgotten about them in this on-going war. Thank you and continue with the good work.

Simper Fi,

Jimmy L. 2nd Lt USMC

May No Soldier Go Unloved

Dear Angel,

We wanted to write you a letter and thank you so very much for your thoughtful Holiday letter. We were touched by your kind words and thoughtfulness in thinking of us so far away from friends, family, and the country we love this Holiday season. We wanted you to know a little about us. We are the 67th Combat support hospital, a field hospital similar to the 4077th MASH from the famous TV series. We care for our soldiers and the local nationals who need immediate life-saving care, stabilizing them, and evacuating them to Germany of the United States for continued care. We have doctors, surgeons, nurses, a full laboratory staff, a dentist, pharmacist, and many very hard working medics, a staff that saves lives every day. While we are based in Germany, we come from all corners of the United States. We are so proud to be taking care of our soldiers while they are defending our great nation. We are grateful to be defending citizens like you who appreciate the sacrifices made by our loved ones, the sacrifices we make to help protect our blessed nation and maintain the freedoms we so dearly love. We hope you will con-

51

tinue to support our nation by being involved in the things that help make America strong: supporting measures that protect and strengthen our families, supporting our children's education, the safety of our communities. We urge you to vote, if you can, and to let your elected representatives know how you feel on the above issues, and other issues important to you and your family. And we urge you to remember our many unsung heroes at home, this season and always: school teachers, firemen, policemen, garbage men, postal workers, and so many countless unsung-all working their hardest to make our nation the greatest on the earth. Many who send us letters and packages want to know what happens to your letters and packages you send. Each letter is read, and every package and letter is gratefully received. The items in packages are given to those most in need, from our unit, to our patients, and to other units who live here in Mosul with us. Many also wanted to know when their letters will be answered. Honestly most letters will not. We, like many soldiers, are very busy and we spend much of our free time either writing to our friends and family, or doing the things to take our minds off of the death and dismemberment we deal with every

day. However, all of your letters are still very much appreciated.

We know that the time and effort you have put into them have

made you a better person, and they reflect all that is great about

America: so many people are concerned enough about their fel-

lowman that they make a significant effort to reach out and love

and help those around them. And your letters, although often

unanswered, really do lift our spirits. We enjoy your stories from

home, knowing about yourself, your family, your ideals; it helps

put a face on the people we are defending. We love your comic

strips, the jokes, the pictures, and everything else you send us.

Please don't feel that if you fail to make a pen pal or fail to re-

ceive a correspondence that your efforts were in vain.

Everything you do makes a difference to us. And we urge you to

continue to reach out to others, not just the soldiers, although we

love you and are grateful for you, but to those in need in your

own communities: the sick, the homeless, the discouraged, the

lonely. Many want to send packages and look for guidance. Eve-

rything we receive is used by someone, so anything you send is appreciated. What do we need? Truly, most of us need very little.

However, there are lots of little things that soldiers enjoy receiv-

ing: batteries, gum, candies, cookies, ets...Books to read, old

magazines to look at, videos, and DVDs, anything to make our

"house" here seem a little more like home. During the holidays

Christmas music is appreciated, as are decorations. Towards the

New Years and Valentines, things to send home to loved ones

are welcomed: again, we don't have a Target or Wal-Mart to

make purchases that remind our loved ones at home how impor-

tant they are to us. Unfortunately, we are not involved with

rebuilding schools or infrastructure here, but there are many

units that are if you wish to send item's to help re-build Iraq.

Rest assured that everything you send us, whatever it may be, is

appreciated. We are thankful people like you who look beyond

themselves to find others to love and support. That willingness to

care for each other is what makes our nation the greatest in the

world. May your holiday season be filled with joy and giving this

year!

Thank you again for all you are doing to support us and our families while we are away.

CPT David K. and all the soldiers of the 67th Combat Support Hospital.

Seasons Greetings Patti and Staff!

I want to thank you for the support and encouragement. It is fascinating to know that strangers from back home care so much about us to take their time and money and mail us a bit of home here in Iraq. Rest assured that every item you have sent was distributed and will be used or consumed. Nothing will go to waste! We appreciate your sentiment and it is because of Americans like you that keep our spirits up through the holidays. The amount of support we receive from home is phenomenal and we will forever be grateful to have such caring people show the patriotism and concern for our country and well being. I look forward to corresponding with you and would like to provide you a copy of my weekly newsletters published in a local Southampton, N.Y. My newsletter varies in subject matter and provides a summary of different events that may be released

Letters From Soldiers

(operational security limits some information) to the general

public. I would be more than happy to forward you a copy every

week via email. If you have a email account, please contact me

so I can send you my first five columns. In addition to the news-

letter, I am organizing a pen pal program for the soldiers in my

company and Americans back at home. I will attach (via email)

a list of soldiers and their gender that would like a pen pal back

at home. This list is available to anyone interested in participat-

ing. I have received numerous letters requesting information as

to what we do over here. A list is being compiled and available

to anyone who wishes to receive one. We could appreciate a

photo of your family and/or yourself so we may hang it next to

your greeting card. This makes your messages personal and also

draws the attention of all the soldiers passing through my office.

We are a medical company from Fort Hood, Texas serving in

Camp Cuervo, in the Ar Rustimayah district of southeastern

Baghdad, Iraq. We have been here since March 2004 and

scheduled to return in a few more months. There are 80 soldiers

in our company (50 medics). We are responsible for treating

May No Soldier Go Unloved

American, Iraqi, and coalition force casualties, and to provide routine clinical care 24 hours a day, 7 days a week. We have been very fortunate thus far as no one from our company has lost their life. We are looking forward to going back home in the next few months and reuniting with our family and loved ones and leading a somewhat normal life. My intent is to build a strong support network for not only the soldiers in this company, but for the Unit that will be replacing us in the near future. They will need all the support they can get as I remember when we first arrived here. We greatly appreciate the warm greetings and thoughtful message you sent us and wish you and your family a happy and safe holiday. You are in our thoughts and prayers.....HAPPY HOLIDAYS!

Sergeant Shawn W. E Co, 115th FSB, 1CD

Letters From Soldiers

Dear Patti,

I would like to thank you for the care packages you sent me. It makes your day when you receive one. I have currently taken on a new position in Shindand, Afghanistan. It is on the Western front near the Iranian border. The mission there is important just as everywhere else in this country. I currently work as an Intelligence and Logistics Mentor for the Afghan National Army. It is a great job I have and spending time and working with the Afghan Officers is always very interesting. This military has come a long way and they truly want to be able to protect their own people from the tyranny of the Taliban. We have taken many strides to create a self sufficient military here in Afghanistan. In our location we currently have about 4,000 school aged children. When we go on our presence patrols throughout the area we are bombarded by children who constantly ask for pens and notebooks for their schools. The schools have been built but the supplies have not been provided or have been all used up. If you do decide to send another care package send the much needed school supplies for the children in the surrounding vil-

lages. The soldiers are pretty well equipped with all they will ever need but the children are truly the future of Afghanistan and supplying school supplies for these kids is probably the most important thing right now. Thank you again for your generosity and the time you took to send the package. I apologize for the time it took me to respond but things have been busy here. Ramadan has been a saving grace for us and slowed things down here dramatically.

Thank You,

Mehdi A. K. S2/S4 Mentor 2/1/207th

Dear Ms. Patti Bader,

Thank you Thank you Thank you, for the shampoos and conditioner's I was so excited to get my package. My Marines were so happy and grateful for your gift. I wish that I could completely explain in words how grateful my heart is. Thank you so much. Well, I was surprised to get your package in the mail. Are you my Angel? I'm not exactly sure how this program goes but I just wanted to let you know a little about myself since I am not sure if you're my official sponsor but I know for sure that you are an Angel. I am 21 yrs old (almost 22) and I joined the Marine Corps when I was 18. I joined because I wanted to make a difference and do my part. I don't regret joining at all I have learned a lot from these Men and Women. At 20 I got married and I just had a little girl. That is definitely the hardest part of this deployment. My daughters name is Madison. She is the reason my husband are able to smile everyday. After almost 2 years of marriage my husband and I have spent 6 months together. He was out here (in Iraq) right before I came out here. He was home 11 days before I came out. He deploys again before I get back. But I am hoping I will run into him while we're both out. Uhm, there really isn't too much to say about out here. The weather has been getting colder, but usually only in the mornings and at nights. The shampoos and conditioners are really coming in handy because for some reason we aren't getting our supplies in. We had a really nice new "chow hall" for dinner but it has been burnt down. So now we have one that everyone goes to so it gets kinda crowded. Oh, the sunsets here are beautiful.

May No Soldier Go Unloved

And today we had a sandstorm. Not everyone likes them but I do.

It so neat to see because sand is everywhere and you can't even

see 30 ft. away. I'm sorry for just going on and on, but I thought

I'd say a little and when I looked the little was longer then I

thought. Ma'am, I just wanted to tell you thank you so much for

the shampoo. I wish you knew what it truly meant when I got to

hand them out.

Thank you, thank you, thank you.

Lila M. CPL USMC

Letters From Soldiers

Dear Patti Patton-Bader:

Hello from Iraq. I want to take this time to express my sincerest appreciation for your wonderful words and act of support. You helped to ease the difficulty of a year-long deployment, and I am eternally grateful. Please forgive the formalness of a typed letter, but my handwriting is poor and illegible. As we have only met through words, I will describe what we do. We are combat engineers stationed in Germany, and we now call Balad, Iraq, home. It is located about 70 miles north of Baghdad. We conduct a multitude of missions to include construction to make the quality of life for Soldiers and Airmen better. We also look for and remove the improvised explosive devices known as IEDS on the major roadways. We have some incredible equipment to protect our combat engineers. I am a husband and father of three children. The family is living in our permanent home in Virginia. The smartest thing we did was purchase before the housing boom. I can not wait until my return to catch up on projects. Our mission is wrapping up, and I will leave Iraq on 4 July – how appropriate. It is a strange feeling because we obviously want to leave, but there was also joy to include job satisfaction. Building

schools and health clinics along with interacting with the most

grateful children I have ever met will be the most rewarding

memories that I will cherish. Again, thank you for your kind

support. May God bless you, your family, and the great Ameri-

cans that have shared their thoughts and kindness. You will

always have a friend in the 130th Engineer Brigade.

Respectfully,

Joe R. LTC HQ, 130th Engineer Brigade

Patti,

Thank you for your time, effort, money and thoughts that went

into the packages you sent this ship. This was the first Christmas

away from home for many of these young sailors and to receive

gifts, cards and "very useful" items from :the folks back home"

made life a little easier out here for them. We are all proud to be

serving our country and helping to protect people like you.

Thanks,

Command Master CMDCM (SS/DV) USS Rentz FFG 46

Letters From Soldiers

Dear Ana Marie Smith and Patti Bader

How are you? I am doing well. It has been about 140-150 degrees here. So I am trying to stay out of the heat as much as possible. That can be a hard when we have work to do. The insurgents don't go out because of the heat they wait toll early morning of night to plant bombs and things of that nature. It has been great your support and caring. I am grateful there are people like you in the world to support and help us troops. To take the time and resources necessary is great boost in morale to know that people do care. The family is doing well missing me but doing well. I will be glad to be home soon. We gotta go for now. Thank You.

Sincerely,

SPC B. ACO 1-187 3ʳᵈ Brigade Combat Team 101ˢᵗ Airbourne

May No Soldier Go Unloved

Dear Mrs. Bader,

Thank you so much for the wonder care package for my squad and me. We all greatly appreciate it from the bottom of our hearts. God Bless You for your support and patriotism for your United States Marines. My name is Ted B. I am 20 years old originally from North Texas. I am married to my outstanding beautiful wife Kenna (also 20) We live at Kaneohe Bay Hawaii where I am stationed. Before the Corps, I was a paramedic at age 18. I loved my line of work, but I have always believed that being a young able man, it is my duty to do something for my country. So, here I sit on my 2nd combat deployment in 2 years and couldn't be more satisfied. I am supposed to get out of the Marines in March 08, but will probable re-enlist depending if I become a father before then. ("Insha Allah" – Arabic meaning God willing). I am an infantryman with the 3rd Battalion, 3rd Marines, LIMA Company, 1st Platoon, 3rd Squad. I am our Squad's combat lifesaver (medic) by approval of our C.O. We don't even take a corpsman out with us on patrols b/c I am as trained as them. Well, I've got some more letters to get done so I *have to wrap this one up. Thank you so much for everything you*

do for us. God Bless You and God Bless America!

Semper Fidelis,

Ted B. LCPL/USMC OIF 3/3 L CO 1ˢᵗ PLT

Dear Soldiers Angels,

I don't know to whom I am writing to but please accept my

thanks for all the wonderful things you do for us who are de-

ployed. In a personal level I'd just like to tell you that, after ten

months in Iraq, I wish I had written earlier and much more often

to your org. As you may already know care packages and letters

can lift anyone's moral despite how tired and hungry he/she may

be. Although this letter may be short please, again, accept our

thanks. Our words may be lacking but our appreciation is not.

Truly,

Sgt Carlos A 1-15 CAV, 101ˢᵗ ABN (AASLT)

May No Soldier Go Unloved

Dear Soldier Angels,

I have had a few humbling moments in a short time I have been in Iraq. Things that just make me stop and be thankful. Today I received another package from your organization. To my surprise, when I opened it I found 50 neck coolers. My jaw dropped and my first thought was I can out fit the whole EQ platoon. (Equipment support) I am in an engineering company. We are the HSC and only have one line platoon. They work long hours in full gear in the hot sun. The fix holes in the road left by IED explosions. They clear roads from litter and trash making it easier to spot IED's. They can build all sorts of things and have some big equipment. The platoon is constantly over worked. I know this because I work in the office and I am there to see them off as they leave for a mission and I am there to welcome them back. But usually hours or even days go by before they return. I received the package late in the day and could not wait till the next day so I could pass them out. First thing in the morning I headed down to the motor pool and showed the other Sergeants what I had and asked them to hand them out to their soldiers. I

Letters From Soldiers

told them about Soldiers Angels and most were very excited. Just the fact someone would think of us makes most soldiers excited. I wondered around passing the rest out to soldiers that I know work outside a lot. Some of the drivers and the mechanics. Some of the soldiers already had one, some have never seen them before. But everyone was interested in what I was carrying. Anytime someone walks around with an open box, it tends to draw attention. Currently I have 3 left. They went fast and everyone who wanted one, got one. I wanted to tell you thank you for what you do. I know you spend your days writing letters and sending boxes, and that is your way of saying thank-you to us. I want you to know that your efforts are also important to this war. It is people like you that keep the soldiers spirit high. Any time a soldier gets a package, they always share. It makes grown men and women turn and go "ooooh goodies!"

Thank you for all you do.

From all of us at HSC EN BN

SGT Julie R HSC 62nd EN BN

May No Soldier Go Unloved

Dear Patti Bader,

Thank you for everything you sent out to us. The coffee and tea are great. The Army seems to run out of coffee some times. It is awesome to get mail here. I'm going to make sure that everything gets to the soldiers who need it. I think all will enjoy a nice cup of joe. I am a Champlain Assistant, which means I work for and with the pastor of our unit. We travel around a lot to provide church and counseling for all the soldiers in 1-36 Infantry. We've been staying fairly busy. This is now my second Deployment to Iraq. In between those, my wife and I have gotten to travel all over Europe. I am 22 years old, married for almost three years now, I met my wife in San Diego at a church youth group. She now lives in Germany, where we are stationed. We are both born and raised in San Diego. We miss the beach, weather, and family. She is misses the shopping, although, it is good to have a home, no matter where it is. Once again thank you for your support. It's good to know there are still Americans out there who still believe in the soldiers out here. I will make sure that the soldiers get everything. The photos are of me and

*my wife in Germany and the Chaplain and I in Iraq with some
local kids. Thank you for all your support.*

Thank you,

SPC Nicholas P. TF 1-36 IN, Camp Hit

Mrs. Bader:

*I want to say thank you very much for your gifts. They were
shared with some very needy children. If you could only see the
smile on their face when we gave them your gift. We would have
our translator tell them where they came from. This support you
give creates a wonderful bond between them and us U.S. soldiers. Thank you so much the gift is appreciated.*

*1LT Rita S. 16th Military "Police" Task Force 134 HHC 16th MP
BDE (ABN)*

Dear Patti,

*I wanted to thank you for being involved with the Soldiers An-
gels. I have received many wonderful letters from people I don't
even know. One Angel was extra special and sent lovely packages of much needed supplies. I want to let you know that I will*

be departing this country of sand soon and heading back to the good "ole U.S. of A." My departure date, although not in just yet, is around the 2nd of May 2006. We will spend a few cays at our DEMOB site in Virginia then it's back, reunited with our families once again. I guess I'll have to mow the lawn again. Oh well HA HA HA! Anyway, thank you and thanks to all the wonderful Angels. You all have been a GOD send. It lifts the heart to know so many people...strangers...care those of us who serve the RED WHITE & BLUE. With Great Admiration,

HTZ Stephen M. S. Navelsf Forward Charlie/DSS Kuwaiti Naval Base Kuwait

Dear Angels and Company C Supporters,

We would like to send a special thank you and have enclosed an Appreciation Certificate for those that have supported our soldiers while deployed in Iraq. Our year in Iraq has finally come to an end and we will be headed home shortly. We thank you all for your support throughout the year. We set a record at the Post Office for having the most mail received in AO North. When sol-

Letters From Soldiers

diers didn't get letters from home, everyone answered their call and wrote to these soldiers. We received everything we could dream of for support and to make our lives comfortable out here. We even had Dryer hoses sent to enhance our laundry room we built. We suffered the devastating Suicide Bombing in our Dining Facility four days before Christmas, but with everyone's support we were able to count our blessings and we had enough stockings filled with goodies to give every soldier at least one and most soldiers two stockings, so they could still enjoy the Holiday Season. We received plenty of personal Hygiene items, phone cards, games, and thoughtful letters. The food we received came in very handy when the Dining facility was shut down due to the bombing. We have been one of the fortunate Companies in our Battalion and will be returning with all our soldiers. We had 10 soldiers receive the Purple Heart Award for injuries sustained in Combat from the Enemy. Most of these were not life threatening and the soldiers had a full recovery. We are anxious to get back home to our state of Maine. By the time everyone gets this letter, we should be back at home enjoy-

ing time with our families, and we can't wait.

So again, thanks for all of your support and if you still want to

contact us our new company address will be:

SSG Eric R. Co C 133d ECB(H) Mosul, Iraq

Dear Patti,

My name is Staff Sergeant Thomas C. As you know, I am cur-

rently deployed to Iraq. I am 30 years lod (31 on the 26th) and

have been in the Army for just over 9 years. I am the Platoon

Sergeant and an OH-58 Delta Kiowa Warrior maintenance pla-

toon. My home base is Schofield Barracks, Hawaii. I have been

married for a little over 7 years and I have two children. They

are my greatest fans. I was born and raised in Boston, Massa-

chusetts. I lived there until just after my 22nd birthday. I joined

the Army just after the first of the year in 1997. People often ask

me why I joined the Army. It is an easy answer. "For as far back

as I can remember I wanted to be a soldier." Of course I had

aspirations to be a professional athlete. However we all know how that turns out. I went to Basic training at Fort Sill, OK.

From there I went to Fort Benning, GA where I learned to jump

out of airplanes. Next I was off to North Carolina. After a couple

of years there I changed my job from a Cannon Crew Member to

a helicopter Mechanic and was stationed at Fort Bragg, North

Carolina. I was then selected to be an Army Recruiter back in

Massachusetts. I recruited for 4 years and 3 months and then

was granted a gift from the gods, Hawaii!!! I spent 10 wonderful

months in Hawaii and then deployed to the largest beach with no

water. (The Desert). I am scheduled to be here until July ??,

2007. It is not as bad as I've heard, but is it ever? I am here with

wonderful soldiers and great leaders. We are all trained to be

the best fighting force in the world. We will not let you down. I

received your package and I wanted to thank you. There is noth-

ing in the box that will go unused. I also want to thank you for

the support you are giving me. It is hard to express the joy I re-

ceive with each correspondence. It means a lot to me that you

care. I pass on to my soldier's everyday that there are people

like you that still believe in us. I wake up everyday and tell my-

May No Soldier Go Unloved

self "I am not fighting for the people of Iraq. I am fighting for the people back home. I am fighting for those who cannot fight themselves. To keep the streets of America terrorist free. I fight the war on terror for my family, my friends and for you. It is my honor...I will be honorable." It motivates me thru the day. I look forward to hearing from you again. I will write as much as possible. I have pictures of my soldiers and I will send to you as soon as I can. They will be sent in "snail mail" as soon as I get a printer to print them. I would email them but my internet access is very limited. Again, thank you for the support you give.

Your American Soldier,

SSG Thomas C. Delta Troop 2/6 CAV

Letters From Soldiers

Dear Soldiers Angels,

Thanks for the care packages and letters that were sent to my company. They were very thoughtful. I think your organization will make the holiday seasons great. The box I received had lots of pocket sized snacks that were perfect for the road. I put them in little baggies with the other treats for those going out on mission a few days. Snacks keep Soldiers awake. There are a few Soldiers in my platoon that do not get much mail. I think they would like receiving something. Their names are listed below. Their address is the same as mine. Thanks again for the goodies! Have a great Holiday season. Sincerely,

Kristina L. W. 146 1ˢᵗ CBT HET, MAINT PLT FOB SPEICHER

May No Soldier Go Unloved

Ms. Patti Bader,

I wanted to write you back to tell you thank you for the package
you sent me. It was greatly appreciated. I was able to share
some of the shampoo with some of the soldiers I am here with.
They too, said thanks. Things here haven't been too bad at all,
and when we get packages and letters from such supportive peo-
ple as yourself, we feel that much more appreciated. Thanks for
the support. If you have the opportunity to send anything else; I
would appreciate some; Cheez-It's, Circus Animal Cookies, and
some candles. Again, thanks for your support.
Peace,
SPC Danielle S. HHC 2 BSB 2 BCT 2 ID FOB Rustamiyah, Iraq

Hello to all my friends and supporters!

First, let me say on behalf of everyone here at the Besmaya
Range Complex, THANK YOU!!! I never, in my wildest dreams
thought there were so many people who were so committed to
those of us deployed in the Combat Zone. I received an Over-
whelming response from all of you and it has renewed my faith

77

and helped me to remember why I asked to come back here

again. It is because of good people like you.

Back in the real world, I am just your average Joe, no different

then any other person on the street. Here, the men and women

who put on the Uniform make a difference, not only to those that

we come in contact with here, but also for those of you at home.

Know that our commitment to you all is there and that what we

do here is worthwhile and has purpose. All the sacrifices, pain

and loss that is reported on CNN cannot compare to all the

worthwhile things we do here. From teaching Iraqi soldiers how

to defend their own country to helping a child get to the US for

an operation (thank you Cerise) to getting things that would take

the whole deployment to get so I can better take care of a village

of people and my own soldiers (Thank you Al, Susan, Lisa n.,

Lynn & Jill E.).

Now about the Packages we have received, our mail comes from

another base, about 45Km west of us. The route has a few pit-

falls so on average we get mail about every 1- 1 ½ months. It

has to come in a re-supply convoy (we call it a LOGPACK),

which is most often our food, fuel and water. I received 6 pallets

of boxes 2 days ago. Our Internet was down, but one of the

things that was in the last box was a router and as you can see

its up and running now fine. I spent the past two days unpacking,

sorting and repacking boxes and supplies. The medical stuff is

here with me, (thank you for the exam gloves, I had used up my

last pair last week and was using surgical gloves, so timing was

wonderful!) The food is in the chapel, along with all of the bath

and hygiene stuff, socks and t-shirts. Coffee and coco are in the

Mess facility along with all of the Christmas stockings, Christ-

mas tree, games and movies. I admit I kept one tray of

homemade fudge for my self, it was just too good, but the other I

did put in the chow hall. I contacted the mail room today, they

say as of right now I have 35 more boxes waiting for me and I

assume from some of the emails that I received while the net-

work was down that I will have a few more added to that

number. I have given out all the MACH 3 razors, we are good to

go for now with those, (my face is thankful for that) but we could

use some shave cream to go with them! So many people have

given so much, not only in donated goods, but also in time, research and out of pocket expenses. So many people who really opened their hearts and though about what we needed and would like (Dave & Cyndy A. the O. family) and all of you, I just want to say thank you. This will be the 16th Christmas I have been away from my family in the past 20 years. This year I have a new family of friends and you all mean as much to me as my own flesh and blood. Thank you for everything you have done for my men and me. I will try to keep you updated as time allows. I wish I could write to each of you, but I will reply to those of you that write me back (I finally am getting the hang of Outlook). If for whatever reason you do not hear back from me before Christmas, I wish you all a wonderful time and blessings on your family.

With warmest regards,

Arthur L. Luneau

SGT/NYARNG

May No Soldier Go Unloved

Patti Bader

I am Sgt. Mike M., the Chaplain Assistant for the 260th Military Intelligence Battalion stationed in Iraq. I received the shampoo and conditioner sent through Soldiers Angesl. Thank you very much. The female soldiers have greatly appreciated it. It is hard to find good quality hygiene items here. Your generosity and support and welcomed and appreciated. Thank you very much. God Bless and take care.

Sgt Mike M. HHSC 260th MI BN

Dear Patti,

I'm sorry it has taken me so long to get back to you. I feel really bad about it. I wanted to thank you for the ink cartridge you sent me. I know it was probably an odd thing for a Marine in a combat zone to ask for but as much printing out as it seems I have to do and as hard as it's been to get ink out here, it was a real blessing. I have the only working copier in the maintenance department. We have a real big one but they run out of toner for it and I can't get more. The outpouring of support from everyone

81

back in the states has been unbelievable. I have received hardly anything from my family and friends (in most cases nothing) and the fact that complete strangers take the time to send us things just says so much and it really warms my heart. I'm so looking forward to coming home next month! I've never been prouder to be a Marine and I look forward to walk around strutting in my dress blues while I am on leave back in Texas and letting the whole world know who I am and what I do. Things are coming to a close here rapidly. In about a month, we are sending the first wave of Marines back home to get things ready for the rest of us going home so we can go right back to work. We are all getting the opportunity to take some well-deserved vacation time when we get back. As soon as we get back, we are automatically getting four days off also which is going to be very nice. It's going to be nice to work a normal work day instead of working 12+ hours a day seven days a week and actually have a weekend off. Well I need to get back to work. Take care and thanks again!
Sgt Wallace E. VMAQ-3 TOOLROOM Unit 78006

May No Soldier Go Unloved

Dear Soldiers Angels,

I am a Airborne Infantryman in the 82nd Airborne Div. I want to say thank you for the packages that we all have been receiving. It really means a lot. Back home not a lot of people agree with what we do over here. People don't understand that this is our job and we do it because someone did it before us to give us the freedoms we have. I just want to do my part to give the next generation the same rights as I had as a child. A little about me, I'm 22 yrs. Old and I'm from Walla Walla, WA. I joined the Army in 2005. I'm very proud to serve in the 82nd ABN DIV. I am a 3rd generation paratrooper for my family. Again, thank you very much. All you do is greatly appreciated. Thank you.

Sincerely,

Pfc Cody H. #5936 HHC 325 STB 2 BCT 82nd ABN DIV Camp-Taji, Iraq

Dear Patti Bader,

My name is SSG Michael M. I am currently in Iraq with the 240th MP CO attached to the 759th MP BN under the 89th MP

Letters From Soldiers

BDE. I am writing to thank you for your participation in the Soldiers Angels program. More to the point I am writing to personally thank you not only for your personal participation, but also for the huge box of snacks and socks. I was able to distribute the socks within my platoon and company. The socks were a big hit, as you can always use socks here. Especially since the warmer weather is approaching. I am extremely surprised at the outpouring from the Soldiers Angels organization and its members. Reading the paper or watching the news lately, I would have thought the general public was against us. It's very nice to see that, although not everyone agrees with the why and where of our troop's deployments, at least they agree to support the troops. Thank you again for taking the time, expense, and thought that went into sending the snacks and socks, they are much appreciated. Please let the others involved with not only the above identified packages, but the entire Soldiers Angels network that we appreciate your efforts.

Respectfully,

SSG Michael C. M. MP Battle NCO 240th MP

May No Soldier Go Unloved

Dear Patti and Jeff

I want to say thank you and I appreciate all that you have done for me. I was overjoyed when I got my shoes, coin and pin. I couldn't believe how fast they got here. I am truly blessed and a better person for knowing you folks. I have decided to pass on the cards like Jeff told me. I chose some single soldiers who could use a morale boost. You have certainly lifted my spirits and those around me. I can not lie to you folks; this duty is the hardest thing I have ever been through by far. It has shaped me into a new man and I have a deep appreciation for my friends and family. If you guys ever need me and I am not in the desert please feel free and call on me. You have a friend with me.

Thank you so much and God Bless "The Soldiers Angels".

SPC B. TRN/OPS/CBRN NCO

Letters From Soldiers

Dear Ms. Bader:

*Thank you so much for the generous support you have shown my battery. We recently received a great box with coffee beans and a grinder as well as a care package of goodies from you. I can tell you, my Paratroopers are routinely surprised by the mail that comes from people such as yourself whom we have absolutely no affiliation with. Those random acts of kindness boaster our belief that regardless of what is in the paper and on TV, the American people still believe in us and support us. Without that our job here would be much more difficult. I read in a letter in your goodie package that you are the founder of Soldiers Angels. Please allow me to extend a special thank you for organizing such an outstanding organization! I logged onto a couple sites such as Adopt a ****** and ****** for Troops as well. Yours is the only organization that just started unloading support on us. The other sites all wanted each individual trooper to log on and register before they could do anything for us. Not that that is a bad thing, but unfortunately that is just not possible where we are. I think the way you have established your organization is* *much more command friendly to allow commanders to set up support for their troops. I have probably received no less than 5 postcards, 8 letters and 5 individual care packages for the guys in addition to what you sent. We even received enough coffee cups with Soldiers Angels emblems on them to give one to each trooper from another one of your Angels. All of that has gone down to the troops who are now started writing and making friends with you folks. I can not say enough about your organization to my higher command. I think you all are special and mean so much to us here.*

Let me tell you a little bit about myself and my battery. I am the commander of an artillery battery based out of the 82nd Airbourne Division at FT. Bragg, NC. I have been in command of the outstanding unit for a year now and I have been at FT. Bragg for almost seven of my eight years in the army. I have deployed to Kosovo, Afghanistan and now Iraq. Being a part of the 82nd Airbourne means we all volunteered to jump out of perfectly good airplanes routinely. I believe the fact that we all volunteered for this duty makes the men of the Division a unique *breed of men willing to do more and do it better. When not deployed we jump on the average of once a month, often at night, and shoot our howitzers and conduct training. Being artillerymen we normally are responsible for shooting howitzers, more commonly called cannons, in support of the Infantry. However, in Iraq there is not much need for that so except for a few of the men we are doing an Infantry mission. We walk the streets, patrol and fight like a standard Infantry Soldier. I have just over 100 men and I truly believe that I have the finest men the nation has to offer under my command. Over half of them have deployed to Iraq not once, but twice before; once for the invasion and again for election support in 2004, as well as supported the Hurricane Katrina Relief efforts. They are all well trained, strong willed, determined, committed and honorable men and I am lucky to be counted among their numbers. Over half of my Paratroopers are single. The average age of my Paratroopers is 22 and they come from all 50 states to include Samoa and the Philippines. During my command three have received their US citizenship. Like I said, my unit is made up of a diverse group of outstanding men. We received word on about the 27ᵗʰ of Decem-*

ber we would be coming to Iraq to take part of the Presidents

Surge force. On the 3ʳᵈ of January we landed in Kuwait to con-

duct some basic training specific to Iraq operations. Within two

weeks we were headed north into Baghdad. We started our Iraq

trip at a large Forward Operating base called Camp Taji. It was

very nice and built up. We had mattresses to sleep on, hot show-

ers, three hot meals a day, gyms and internet access. We spent a

lot of our Taji time training and really getting good at those In-

fantry missions we would be asked to do. Then in early

February, practice time was over and we headed out into our

sector of Baghdad for game time. We have now established

Camp War Eagle in North Baghdad. This is nothing like Taji.

We set this up ourselves from scratch. When we rolled in here

the first night we treated it if it were filled with bad guys. Make

no mistake; we all realize we are in bad guy country now. We

operate in sector mounted in special up-armored trucks as well

as dismounted by walking the streets. Unlike what the media has

painted as the picture of Iraq, I would say we are making a lot of progress here. The majority of the people are glad we are here and embrace us. Some of the people are ready for us to leave here but they don't cause any problems. Most of the people are like you and me and want a safe, secure place to live. Iraq is by no means a safe place to be yet. We face the threat everyday. There are some bad people here who do bad things – both to their fellow Iraqi as well as to us. We are here to find those people and show them what happens when you do bad things to good people. Our living conditions are nothing like what we had in Taji. I would say that in all my army experience this is probably the most austere location I have been. Mail runs about one time per week and we count on the mail and the logistics that come forward with the mail to sustain us. We live in an old building that was part of a water treatment plan. We have running water a couple hours a day and power most of the day. We have not had a hot meal since we left in early February. We eat Meals Ready to Eat – it is a basic army meal in a bag. Internet is spotty at best though the Battalion satellite that will allow phone usage. At this point most of our effort has gone into improving our security here at the Camp. We do have cots to sleep on now so that is an improvement. I think that is a sign of good things to come. I think the Paratrooper is the most resourceful of all Soldiers. We have already come up with a latrine we can use and I hear the guys are working to put 55 gallon drums on the roof to heat and store water for shaving and showers. Things will unquestionably get better as time goes by. So, that is what we are doing right now and a little bit about what it is like. The Bravo "Bulls" are doing well. Everyone is healthy and working hard to bring security to our sector of Baghdad. If you hear anything about the 2nd Brigade 82nd Airbourne Division or 2-319th Airbourne Field Artillery Battalion on the news – that is us. Thank you again for your support. If your organization wants to send anymore mail or package to the Paratroopers the best way to do it is to send it to me. Please keep our post active on your website and feel free to post my above comments about how much we appreciate it on your site on your behalf. You well know the Army doesn't allow "any soldier mail" anymore and I can not send names back. Like I did with your stuff, when the mail ar-

rives I pass all that out to the boys. On big boxes of stuff that is not separated with individual letters or return address we kind of "divvy up the goods". If they want to adopt a trooper or two please just package separate letters or care packages and send them to me in one mailing and I will get it to them and they can begin to correspond with you directly rather then going through me. You asked what the guys would like or need. Like I mentioned this is pretty austere here. We need the basics: letters, books and magazines, newspapers, baby wipes, toilette paper (the soft kind), homemade goodies, snacks, AA and AAA batteries and sundry items such as soap and toothpaste. Bigger items we use a lot here are the little head lamps and small flashlights. Basically anything people send we appreciate. One of your members sent a baseball hat and team Super Bowl T shirt. Another one sent a nerf football. We love all that kind of stuff. There is really no limit. A year is a long time to be away and when everything you have fits in a duffel bag most things that make it like home here come in the mail. Please keep us in your thoughts and prayers! May God bless you for supporting us and the American Soldier.

All the Way!

Jon H. Commander B/2-319ᵗʰ AFAR 82ⁿᵈ ABN DIV

Edith,

I would like to thank you for the Valentine's card that I received from you. I would also like to thank you for all of the Hero letters that I have passed out to my men. I know for a fact that it made a difference to them. They just happen to come at just the right time too. I am sure that you have probably already heard about the attack that happened in Karbala, Iraq. That was me and my men that were involved in that whole operation. They hit us pretty hard that night. As a unit, we lost 4 men and one Captain that was attached to us for this mission. We lost our Platoon Leader and three other soldiers. Two of them happened to be my men. One of my men is a true Hero. He, without any hesitation jumped on a grenade that was thrown in on us. Because of his bravery, he saved my life and the lives of 3 other soldiers. It is not that often that we have the opportunity to have known a true Hero, and I will always treasure the memories that he has left for us. We have had a hard time coping with the loss of our friends, and the letters put a huge smile on the faces of the men in my Platoon. For this, I can never thank you enough.

I do not know if I have told you how much it means to me that you have been writing. It is so nice to see that there are still some people that are supporting the things that we are doing here. Although I have pretty much stop believing in the whole thing, it is still nice to know that we are being supported. There are so many parents that are turning against their kids for being here. They do not understand the things that the men and women are going through here and they just are so fast to tell them that they have a problem. I have seen this first hand and from that of my soldiers. Well, I have to be going for now. I did get an e-mail from you, but have not had the chance to completely read it. At the time that I got my e-mail opened, they pulled me out saying that we have a problem that I have to attend to. I guess that I should be honored that I am the only one of the bosses out of the 5 that we have here, that they can trust. I

should be able to read it today. God bless. "Greater Love has

no one that this, that one lay down his life for his friends".John

15:13

SSG Billy W. A 2-377TH PFAR

Dear Steve and Ying,

23 July

Hey! How are you? How is life in y'all's neck of the woods? I

got your package today. I have never gotten so many birthday

cards before. I appreciate it very much. I am glad you sent the

letters in a package. 18 letters. That is 140 pushups. I only did

25 for the package. I am gonna have to get a new pen to write to

everyone back. At least when I go to the field I will have some-

thing to do. I really do appreciate what y'all do for me and the

other soldiers. It's a blessing to have people such as you and the

other Angels in the world. Thanks again my friends.

Well, I guess I can tell you about what is going on over here. I

just got back from Baghdad. I had to go to the U.S. Embassy and testify against a guy I caught. He is going to jail. The day I left is when that bomb went off in Iraq that killed so many people. It is the town my patrol base is in. It went off about 500-700 meters away from my patrol base. I tell the guys I leave for 5 days and they act a fool while I am gone. Now I have to straighten these Iraqi's out. I give them no slack. I treat every Iraqi as a possible terrorist. I am coming home to my family and preferably only a few pounds lighter than when I got here. Don't worry! I will be safe. Well while I was in Baghdad I had a small vacation. I swam at the embassy pool everyday. I swam from 7 A.M. to 11 P.M. and only stopped to eat between. I only got burned the last day I was there. I loved not having to wear body armor all day. The embassy is awesome. It was one of Saddam's main palaces in Baghdad.

May No Soldier Go Unloved

25 July

Well today I head back out into the field. I have two new guys going with me. One has been in the country since we got here, but just not outside the wire. The other guy got here last week. This will be there first OP mission. We will be there for a full 5 days. I am gonna work on getting my suntan while I am out there. I got a real bad farmers tan. LOL. I want to thank you again for your support Mr. Steve and Mrs. Ying. I have never before gotten so many birthday cards. I am gonna have plenty to write this week in the field. It is worth it though for nice folks such as y'all.

Letters From Soldiers

26 July

These guys are gonna kill me. I let one of my guys shoot a grenade from his grenade launcher. He was supposed to shoot green smoke and instead shot a green flare that bounced off the target back at us and illuminated the whole area in the middle of the night. My heart skipped a few beats. First from the ricochet and then from the flare. My soldiers are driving me crazy. LOL. Well, let me let you go. Take care for now. I will talk to you later.

Sincerely Your Friend in Iraq,

David E. C III Sgt C75 B Co 1/155 Infantry B TN 155 BCT

May No Soldier Go Unloved

Hi there,

Happy Halloween to you and your family too. I'm still here, waiting to receive word as to when we roll out. I have gotten the word but of course I can't say when. It's been delayed due to the bad weather but it's imminent. I have chosen two of my soldiers to go with me, the rest will wait for our return from a safe location. Many feelings have come over me as we prepare for the largest and most dangerous ground assault ever attempted in Iraq. I'm not the real religious type, and I haven't "found" God because I fear I will meet him soon. I pray for our safe return and for strength as a leader. My soldiers understand why I have chosen them from the rest and they will follow me into battle. I always lead from the front and do all I can to keep them safe. The three of us will keep the tanks in the fight for as long as we can. Of the eight, they all wanted to go with me, but unfortunately, some must stay back to keep this place safe. I can't tell you exactly where we are going, but I'm sure that CNN has put out enough information for everyone to figure it out. I chose a prayer from Psalms that I have recited to all of my soldiers, and I pray for their safety in the event things don't turn out as well as I hope. I have put it on the bottom of the page so you can

read it. This will test all my abilities as a person and as a leader, I

know I am ready. This will not be like the everyday combat that goes

on here, the rules of engagement are clear; anyone left in the city is

a terrorist. An ultimatum has been given to which they have not

complied. For the past week they have launched mortars and fired

rockets at us to deter us from going, it's not enough. I know I have-

n't been able to send you that picture I said I was gonna send, but

hopefully not long from now.   I will have to give you a mental pic-

ture of me for now, lol. I am 5' 11" and about 225 Ibs. I have black

hair and brown eyes. I have a mustache too, but not all sloppy,

lol. I keep it short and maintained. My mother is Mexican and my

father is German, but I took mostly from her I guess because I

maintain a good tan, lol. I'm not a go to the gym type person, but I

manage somehow to stay in shape. Guess that's from growing up on

a farm and working with heavy equipment all the time, then and

now. So now, you can maybe picture me somewhat. When you think

of me, put on a big smile and it will find its way to me. I can't even

say thank you enough for what you do, take care and I'll do the

May No Soldier Go Unloved

same. Hope to talk with ya soon,

Troy

The LORD is my shepherd; I shall not be in want.

He follows me through the green pastures,

He leads me beside quiet waters, He restores my soul.

He guides me in paths of righteousness for his name's sake.

Even though I walk through the valley of the shadow of death,

I will fear no evil, for you are with me;

your comfort and love, they protect me.

You prepare a table before me in the presence of my enemies.

You anoint my head with oil; my cup overflows.

Surely goodness and love will follow me all the days of my life,

and I will dwell in the house of the LORD forever.

Pictures From Soldiers

Private First Class Brandon Varn (Al Fallujah Iraq 2003)

M109 A6 Self Propelled Paladin Howitzer (Iraq Syrian Border 2003)

May No Soldiers Go Unloved

Brandon and his Paladin Unit (near Al Asad Air Force Base, Iraq 2004)

Brandon playing a guitar that we shipped him (Al Fallujah Iraq 2003)

Pictures From Soldiers

Brandon and the 4th Infantry rolling in from Kuwait
(just over the Iraqi border April 2003)

Brandon and his Paladin Unit broke down somewhere in the Al Anbar Province, Iraq 2003. Brandon explained, "Had to replace the engine crank and transmission. Can't call the auto club out there."

Home is where you hang your hat. Brandon and his unit slept in their Paladin for the first few months (Al Anbar Province Iraq 2003)

Picture Brandon took on patrol (Al Fallujah Iraq 2003)

Pictures From Soldiers

Picture Brandon took on patrol (Al Fallujah Iraq 2003).

Picture Brandon took on patrol (Al Fallujah Iraq 2003)

Keep your helmet on. On patrol (Al Fallujah, Iraq 2003)

First Class Private Brandon and First Class Private Joshua F.
(near Ar Ramadi, Iraq 2003)

Pictures From Soldiers

Brandon on guard duty with a machine gun and a fly swatter
(outside of Al Fallujah, Iraq 2003)

Back home from Iraq, Corporal Brandon Varn becomes a certified non-commissioned officer at the Primary Leadership Development Course
(Fort Sill Oklahoma 2004)

May No Soldiers Go Unloved

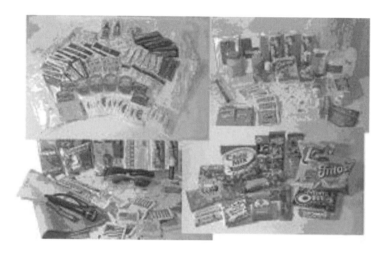

Type of items Soldiers Angels includes in a heroes care package

May no Soldier have the munchies!

Pictures From Soldiers

Holiday cheer for the troops

May No Soldiers Go Unloved

Look at those smiles!

Pictures From Soldiers

Showing off their Soldiers Angels sand scarves

"I'm too sexy for my scarf." The sand scarves and cooling scarves are much appreciated!

Troops Celebrating Christmas (Baghdad Iraq 2003)

Troops Celebrating Thanksgiving (Baghdad Iraq 2006)

Pictures From Soldiers

Soldiers of the 657th celebrate Christmas at Camp Anaconda (Balad, Iraq 2006)

Group portrait F Co 3-25 AVN (Iraq 2007) This company provides Air Traffic and Radar Services for U.S. aircraft in Iraq.

Passing out school supplies to children

Afghani children wearing donated clothes and shoes

Pictures From Soldiers

Soldiers passing out supplies donated by Angels (Iraq 2006)

Soldier providing medical assistance (Iraq 2006)

Pictures From Soldiers

Soldiers Angels and a Blanket of Hope

First Response Backpack and Blanket of Hope

May No Soldiers Go Unloved

Brave heroes showing off their new threads and First Response Backpacks

Medics with First Response Backpacks

Pictures From Soldiers

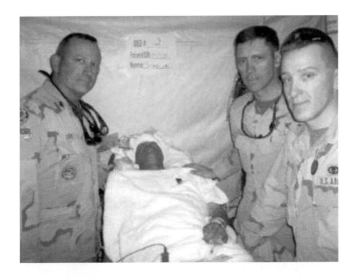

Picture sent to us from a Medivac Unit in Iraq.

Intensive Care Nurse at Lundstuhl Regional Medical Center Germany showing off mittens, socks, and hats donated by a Cub Scout troop of Soldiers
Angels to keep the wounded warm during their long flights in transport
planes back to the States.

May No Soldiers Go Unloved

Wounded Soldiers displaying their First Response Backpacks

Nurse and two happy soldier recipients of First Response Backpacks
(Iraq 2006)

Pictures From Soldiers

Blankets of Hope

Blankets of Hope

May No Soldiers Go Unloved

Soldiers Angels Challenge Coin

Soldiers Angels Pin

Pictures From Soldiers

Fund Raising Strategies Soldiers Angels calendar

May No Soldiers Go Unloved

Soldiers Angels raising funds and awareness

A Soldiers Angels meeting

Pictures From Soldiers

One of the Angels proudly wearing her "colors"

Congressman Adam Schiff and volunteer Angels at a Soldiers Angels
donation booth

May No Soldiers Go Unloved

Political cartoonists John Cox and Allen Forkum's original artwork. After publishing the cartoon in the *Washington Post*, Cox and Forkum put the original artwork up for auction on eBay with proceeds going to Soldiers Angels Valor IT project. The kind gentleman that purchased the artwork donated it to Soldiers Angels

The inspiration of the Valor IT project sent Patti a copy of his (Captain Z. pictured above) Purple Heart and Bronze Star

Pictures From Soldiers

Original Art presented to Soldiers Angels by artist Lei Hennessy Owen who is also working on a Shanksville Memorial.

Metallica Poster unexpectedly sent to Brandon from the famous rock 'n roll poster artist Randy Tuten. Coincidently, the dates of the concert on March 11, 2004 - the exact date Brandon's unit landed on American soil in Bangor, Maine after a year in Iraq

May No Soldiers Go Unloved

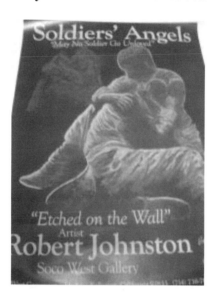

Poster from original painting "Etched on the Wall" by artist and Korean War veteran Robert Johnston. The Soco Gallery in Fullerton, CA. held a fundraising for Soldiers Angels and Mr. Johnston signed copies of the poster and the Gallery owners generously donated the proceeds to Soldiers Angels.

Soldiers Angels wreath ceremoniously placed (with military escort) by two Angels at The Tomb of the Unknown Soldier.
(Arlington National Cemetery in Arlington, Va. 2004)

Pictures From Soldiers

Soldier riders peddling for the ocean

From the Atlantic to the Pacific!

May No Soldiers Go Unloved

Marine Rider and wife

Soldier Rider and wife

Pictures From Soldiers

Volunteer Soldiers Angels at the Soldier Ride San Clemente, California

Blanket made by Soldiers Angels for Soldier Riders

The flag of the Military Order of Purple Hearts flown from the stage at the Soldier Ride

Young Americans making care packages and greetings for the troops

Pictures From Soldiers

Happy bunch of teachers and classmates preparing care packages
for deployed soldiers

5

Here Comes the Kevlary

Patti Patton Bader didn't just wait for problems in Iraq to come to her, she went looking for them. While blogging one morning in October 2003 Patti came across an article about soldiers who were on patrol in the cold, mountainous border region between Iraq and Iran. In the article, a few soldiers were interviewed and described the harsh and frigid conditions under which they were working. Patti wanted to help.

The article mentioned that the highest ranking officer interviewed was named John D. from Houston. Patti searched the Houston phone book and called up *each and every* John D. she could find until she luckily found Capt. John D.'s wife, Mrs. D. This took over three hours and I thought my wife was a little possessed and slightly crazy. Mrs. D. was also a little concerned at first too, but Patti left her references and after Mrs. D. consulted Capt. D. she gave Patti the entire units APO addresses. "They're freezing out there. They need thermal underwear and coffee."

Patti went on eBay and immediately bought 100 pair of long thermal underwear and winter socks. She called a few of the Angels and pounds of coffee were donated and sent, including a few bags from my local Starbucks. A manager at a Lowes Department store was contacted by an Angel and additionally donated clothes and flashlights. Americans are very generous people when they believe a cause is worthy and noble. It seemed like anyone who had heard about Soldiers Angels wanted to help. Patti had thrown a pebble into a pond of patriotism and the ripple caused a tidal wave of good will. Soldiers in Iraq and Afghanistan started to hear about Soldiers Angels and hundreds began joining daily. Soon Chaplains and Platoon leaders in Iraq and Afghanistan started registering the soldiers of their entire Units' APO addresses with Soldiers Angels.

May No Soldier Go Unloved

It seemed every day and sometimes every hour Patti or one of the Angels would find a new cause or someone in need of help. Soldiers Angels was starting to receive specific requests from soldiers in Iraq and Afghanistan. "Could you send a thousand sand scarves to the troops in Al Anbar Province?" "Please send some warm socks and the new White Stripes CD." "Could the Angels send shoes and clothing for the children living in an orphanage in Afghanistan?" A field hospital requested hospital gowns. There was no shortage of needs. The deployed soldiers lacked so many things and Soldiers Angels honored each and every request.

As more aid was requested Patti started different projects and teams. One of the projects which made a significant difference was a project that Patti called "Armor Up."

Patti had discovered that our troops in Iraq were riding in unarmored vehicles while on combat patrol. The Army hadn't intended for Humvees to be used on combat patrols and some of them were equipped with only vinyl doors and aluminum flooring. A stock S.U.V. bought from your local auto dealer provides more protection from sniper fire then some of the Humvees in which our troops were being transported. I remember watching the Secretary of Defense on T.V. as he addressed the troops in Baghdad. He was asked about the lack of body and vehicle armor that the Army was providing to the troops, and said, "You go to war with the Army you have, not with the Army you might want."

Several Angels reported to Patti that their "soldier adoptees" were concerned about their safety while traveling in unarmored vehicles. Patti found a company that distributed police, security, and military equipment. Soldiers Angels started raising money and buying "Kevlar Blankets" to send to Iraq.

A Kevlar Blanket is a special reinforced blanket the troops attach to the doors and floors of their unarmored Humvees and military vehicles. In urban combat where speed is less important, the soldiers would wrap the sides of their vehicles in Kevlar armored blankets for additional protection against sniper fire and in areas where IED's (Intermediary Explosive Devices) were a problem, trucks, Humvees's and APC's (Armored Personal Carriers) used them to line their floorboards. Each Kevlar blanket cost around a thousand dollars but they significantly increased the protection of the troops from I.E.D.'s and sniper fire.

During the first year of Operation Iraqi Freedom, Soldiers Angels sent hundreds of Kevlar Blankets to units on the front lines, before the Army re-armored their vehicles and provided all of our troops with the proper body armor they should have been equipped with originally.

Patti,

Here are the gut reactions from Charlie about receiving the armor blanket: Thank you guys so much for your generosity, this is the action that everyday citizens can take that show how much we are supported from our homes and even from people we haven't met. Although the Government is taking awesome measures to ensure our safety, gifts like this give much more than safety. They also give you security, security that there are people back home that appreciate the sacrifices. Patti, both Charlie's mother Kathy and Linda, Charlie's Aunt, wanted me to pass on their thanks for both your personal donation and the Soldier's

Here Comes the Kevlary

Angels contribution that made it possible to get the Armor Blanket for him. And thanks from me,

Gary

Dear Patti,

You're doing amazing things for these Soldiers here. I can look back when we were shaking in our boots going out in those old trucks, your blankets came in, and the whole world changed that day. Everyone looked sharper, worked harder, and just got a rush of life because we were better protected. Now the trucks that they are making can't even fall under the truck category, because of all the armor and gadgets. We were just hidden on a small camp using old equipment and too many people would have had to travel too many miles to get us the good stuff.

CPT Brian

May No Soldier Go Unloved

Dear Patti,

"Very special thank you. The request for blankets came from a CPT from this unit. He could not return to Iraq with his soldiers because of the extensive injuries to both his legs. He wanted to be sure it didn't happen to any of his fellow soldiers"

Angel Robin B.

"One soldier told me he had seen first hand how a blanket saved his Sgt's Legs and possibly his life. When their vehicle was hit by an IED, a piece of shrapnel came up through the floor and the blanket trapped it and contained it so no harm came to his legs."

Angel Anna Marie S.

"The blankets are awesome. They really allow us to protect our patients better when we have to transport them back to the post. I am very impressed with the quality."

Sgt. Brett P.

Here Comes the Kevlary

Dear Ma'am,

I just want to thank you for all of your hard work and effort to supply myself and my troops with armor. Your efforts will not go unappreciated. It is people like you who make our nation the greatest in the entire world. The commitment and sacrifice that individuals like yourself make to support the soldiers out here in Iraq eases not only the concerns of the soldiers themselves but also the minds of our families and friends back home. I just want to reiterate my gratitude for your wonderful efforts.

Sincerely,

SGT Micheal M.

Little Ripples of Kindness

Patti was the epicenter of the Angels, but the wave of kindness, sacrifice and duty got bigger the farther it emulated. "These little ripples of kindness add up to oceans of greatness," is Patti's mantra. It is truly amazing how Americans responded to Soldiers Angels.

Patti learned of a mother who had a soldier deployed in Iraq. She had been mailing her son care packages outside of a Post Office in Sacramento, California when her car got stolen. The car was later recovered but had been vandalized and trashed. Patti looked up the car dealerships in Sacramento and made one phone call and explained the situation and then called the soldiers mother. The dealership donated the parts and mechanics their labor *for free* to fix the car. When the local alarm company heard about this mom's plight, they installed a state-of-the-art car alarm system into her car *at no charge.*

In another instance, a combat hospital in Iraq asked for aluminum siding, so they could protect the walls of their hospital. A Soldiers Angels volunteer drove to her local Home Depot and explained the situation to the manager. The store took a collection among its employees and the goods were donated. A nurse from Lundstuhl Regional Medical Hospital requested large mittens for the wounded that were being transported back to the States via unheated transport planes. The I.V.'s (intravenous devices) were making it impossible for the wounded to put on their regular sized gloves. Could we send a couple hundred pairs of oversized gloves? A few minutes later a Cub Scout leader called and asked how his troop could help. Within three days, his troops of 10-year-old cub scouts raised enough money to purchase and send 100 pairs of oversized mittens *and booties.* Countless acts of kindness and caring were occurring daily. From sea to shining sea, Soldiers Angels was like a bright warm summer day and it made everyone smile.

May No Soldier Go Unloved

I also found out that Patti was a natural at logistics. She handled hundreds of tasks, big and small, with ease. Patti seemed to revel in Soldiers Angels. Like her great uncle, General George S. Patton., General Patti Patton Bader felt like the stars had aligned and she was the exact right person at the exact right place in the exact right moment of history for this exact job.

For example, Patti seems to naturally have the power to motivate others. One of the first people to call us, Anna Marie S., innocently asked how she could additionally help. She is now President of Soldiers Angels. Anna Marie S. believed so much in the Soldiers Angels mission that before Soldiers Angels became incorporated, she maxed out her and her husband's personal credit cards for supplies on the hope and promise that Patti could raise the funds to pay her back.

Patti's reaction time to problems is also extraordinary. General Patton-Bader moves fast and gets things done. For example, one day near Christmas last year Patti saw a news story called "The Grinch That Stole Marines' Christmas" flash on T.V. A local news station was reporting about a Marine mom in Illinois who spent all her money at Christmas time to buy her son and his unit Christmas presents. The mom wrapped and stored all the presents she bought in her garage but before she could ship them somebody broke in and stole all the presents. This Marine mom was broke and devastated. She couldn't afford to buy more presents and her son would have to go without any this year. Patti quickly looked up the mom on the internet and found her phone number and within a few minutes of the broadcast called her. Patti introduced herself and asked the Marine's mom for the names and addresses of her son's entire Marine platoon in Iraq and immediately sent Christmas care packages out to all of them (She additionally sent the mother some cash).

Like her Great Uncle George, Patti was also an excellent tactician. Patti would find your expertise and utilize it as the needs arose. I'm a musician, and Patti has seen the "healing" power of music, so when a guitar was needed to be presented to a deployed soldier, wounded hero, or military child who had just lost a parent, I was chosen to handle those jobs. I always feel stupid and inadequate presenting a kid with a guitar after he or she has

just lost a parent, but I've gotten back heartfelt and sincere letters of thanks from some of these kids and relatives and it made
me realize that the process of healing has more to do with the
acknowledgement of their loss and the gesture of kindness, then
it has to do with the gift itself or the healing power it contains.
Other Angels volunteered their time for jobs that they were good
at and the avalanche of support from the nation was awe-
inspiring. Americans enthusiastically endorsed the mission and
the concept of Soldiers Angels.

Patti was on a roll, and she called dozens of radio stations and
pleaded for their help in getting her message out. From our bedroom, Patti would conduct radio interviews, answer questions,
and put out a plea for donations and action. She was such a great
radio guest that she was almost always invited back to spread the
gospel of Soldiers Angels. Patti's energy and motivational skills
are amazing and made great radio. It was fun watching the
amount of visitors and donations to the Soldiers Angels website
after one of her radio appearances. After the first couple of
months, radio stations we had never heard of started calling Patti

for interviews. Patti was on the radio so much, even when I would speak with strangers and mention my wife's name, or the Soldiers Angels organization, they would tell me "oh wow, I've heard of her" or "I've heard about those Soldiers Angels." One of my North Carolina clients drawled, "Your wife is famous! I know about her. I heard her on the radio!" It was kind of like living with a celebrity. Patti was so busy I had to start emailing her for "appointments" in order to see her! The first year Brandon was in Iraq, Patti was on the phone so much that she burned out three brand new phone systems. Great Uncle George would have been proud of her.

May No Soldier Go Unloved

Thanks so much for your note Patti! I love my son and he is my

hero! He was on the Oliver North War stories on FOX T.V. last

night. Oliver rode in Kaleb's truck. Kaleb called from Iraq yes-

terday and told us to watch the show. What a wonderful

surprise. I cannot tell you how much those guys appreciated the

food you so generously gave money for. They are a more forgot-

ten group with a little base and don't have the good home cooked

food. You are my heroes too!!!!!

Love,

Mary W. Moline, Il.

Dear Patti,

Just before the awards presentation, a young soldier came up to

me and said did I hear right you are from Soldier's Angels.

When I answered yes, he gave me a hug and said he didn't think

that without Soldiers' Angels, they could have done what was

needed to be done or make it back without our prayers, letters,

thoughts, and packages. It was what kept them going. He went on to say how much Soldiers Angels did for him, his men and especially the kindness and friendship toward his wife was unbelievable. He almost had me in tears. All I could do was hug him back, shake his hand, and tell him thank you. Right after that it was announced that I was there representing Soldiers Angels to accept the award for SA. When Soldiers' Angels was announced, cheering from the soldiers was loud and clear. Fortunately when I was given the award on Soldiers Angels behalf, I didn't have to speak, because my voice would have been shaking for sure. I was able to get the words out thanking the CO, CSM, and all of the 1st Cavalry for the award on behalf of Soldiers Angels.

Angel Linda D.

Dear Ms. Bader:

My name is LCpl. Kaleb J. W. I'm a Marine grunt stationed in Ramadi, Iraq. I'm not sure if you know my mother, Mary W. or not, but I did enclose a list of everyone in my platoon to her. Everyone in my platoon received a package from Soldiers Angels and they were a big hit, especially the logo mugs and coins.

May No Soldier Go Unloved

I wanted to thank you, Soldiers Angels, and everyone else who are supporting us. Your generosity will not be forgotten. It speaks very highly if your character to take time out of your schedule to help us. I pray that this letter, my small token of appreciation and sincerity, reaches you and your loved ones safely, in high spirits and good health. All of the supplies you sent were distributed equally, and any remainders were displayed at the ship store for others to take if they chose. I hope that you and all of our friends, families, loved ones, and supporters a Merry Christmas and a Happy New Year. Feel free to write anytime you wish, and if you have any questions, I will answer them as honestly as liberty permits. God Bless and thank you again.
Sincerely,

Kaleb J. W. 1ˢᵗ BN 6ᵗʰ MAR Wpns. Co. Map 4

The Letter Writing Team

Patti believes soldiers who receive letters of support from home have a better chance of coming home healthy and have a better chance of adjusting back into civilian life with less chance of Post Traumatic Stress Disorder (PTSD). She says that our support and appreciation have healing powers for our returning soldiers. Besides the hero packs, sand scarves, underwear, thermal kits, CDs, DVDs, laptop computers, kevlar blankets, and the kitchen sinks the Soldiers Angels were sending overseas, Patti also wanted every soldier to receive a letter of support at every mail call. We received hundreds of return cards and letters from deployed soldiers, thanking us for these letters, and telling us, "that getting your name called at mail call is kind of like getting a present at Christmas." Patti thought reading these letters was therapeutic for the troops and reminded them we supported their duty and to "do what they had to do" to come home safe.

In May 2004, Patti and Sara E., another military mom, formed the Soldiers Angels "Letter Writing Team" composed of a group of dedicated volunteer Angels that continually write letters of support to our deployed soldiers. Sara E.'s letter writing team is the muscle and bone of Soldiers Angels and really epitomizes the Angel spirit. To date, over 250,000 letters have been mailed to our brave soldiers in Iraq and Afghanistan and continue today at the pace of over 10,000 to 15,000 letters monthly. Several churches, schools and boy scout troops from across this great country have helped the Soldiers Angels Letter Writing Team and the soldiers really seem to enjoy the correspondence from the kids and those letters especially seems to help their morale. In a world of hate and war, a heartfelt letter from an eight-year-old can put a smile on the face of even our most hardened warriors.

The Letter Writing Team

Dear Brave, Courageous American Soldier,

Back in August, I wrote a letter for a Soldiers Angels program which I had learned about through my church. I was both surprised and honored when I received a call asking if it could be copied for our beloved soldiers serving our nation. My heart has been overwhelmingly touched by the stories you all have written back. I admire all of you more then ever!

You are true heroes! Your courage and loyalty make you shining examples of being America's "best"! Your selfless devotion to defending the freedom of others and protecting the world puts you up on a pedestal of greatness.

Please know how much the people of American appreciate what you are doing. Your lives are in constant danger protecting people you don't even know. You are to be admired for completing your task no matter what your assignment is. Each and every one of you is playing a significant role.

I pray for you and your families daily as you are so far away from your loved ones. How they must miss you, yet be so proud of you! They love you with all of their heart. God also loves each and every one of you. He will never leave you or forsake you. He is by your side every moment and with every step you take. His presence is your companion; his love, your protection; and his power, your strength. Count on him – he is your loving and faithful Shepard.

It is an honor and privilege to write to you. America, the land of liberty, is great because of you! I thank God for you in my prayers – for being who you are and for bravely serving your country. During these difficult and challenging times, if you ever feel frightened, lonely, or fogetten, may God's unfailing love sustain you.

God bless you and thank you for faithfully carrying out the job you were called to do.

With Loving appreciation,

Sarah B. Philadelphia, PA.

The Letter Writing Team

To Our Beloved Serviceperson,

On behalf of Calvary Chapel of the Foothills, we would like to express our sincere appreciation of your dedication and servitude to the United States of America. We want to thank you for placing your life on the line for justice, freedom, and the preservation of democracy – it is our hope that God uses you as a conduit for integrity and honor.Please know that the larger voice of American society is praying for you and supports your valiant efforts; so much so that this package has been made possible by the members of this congregation in hopes of sending a small piece of home to the Middle East.

Once again, please accept this small gift as a token of utmost respect and appreciation – we thank you for unselfishly protecting our homeland. May God protect you and bless you richly. Please pass on the rest of the care packages sent in your name to other soldiers.

The Congregation of the Calvary Chapel of the Foothills La-Canada, CA.

May No Soldier Go Unloved

Dear Soldiers Angels,

I wanted to write to y'all and thank you for the care package and letter that I received. It is very appreciated. You guys really uplifted my morale and my spirit. To be honest that was the 1ˢᵗ letter I got since I've been here. I've gotten a couple since from my parents. Y'all have been a big help to me and to my soldiers. Thank You!

Pfc. Joe F. HHC 325 STB 2 BCT 82ⁿᵈ Airborne Div. Camp Tagi

Dear Bradon,

I have a brother named Adrian. He was in the navy. He was in the navy for four years. My brother took pictures of his ship and in his ship. Adrian rode a big ship. The color of it was gray and white. The boys that were in the navy made a flag. My brother made a clown on his flag. When he came back I made a poster that said, "Welcome back Adrian". I missed him.

Brandon what do you, where, when you fight? How many minutes and hours do you fight? Mrs. Butts said that you may be fighting for two days.

Sincerely
Emily. M.
Room #29

East Alexander Middle

Hiddenite, North Carolina
28635
November-18-03

Dear Soldier,
My name is Michael C. I am
12 years old. I have brown hair. I
have horses. I like dogs and
chickens and I like to deer hunt
and play lot's of sport's. My horse
Argybian. She is a mare her
name is Sugar. She is brown
and the best horses I know.
I have a strong feeling about
the war. I don't like it. I
hope all of you Army hurry up
and win the battle.
If you deer hunt, I'd love to
talk with you about hunting. It
is Muzzleloading hunting
season here. I love
Sports like baseball, basketball,
football.
I have the video game

on "Meatle of Honor." It is
a fun game. It tells you
about what has happen in the war.
My family is a big family.
Most of us like to deerhunt,
We all hunt white tail deer
in North Carolina.

your friend
Michael C

PS. write back soon please.

Eight Air Miles High

It's funny how things seem to cosmically work. In September 2003, Patti got a call from a guy in New York named Rich L. who heard Patti on the radio and wanted to help. He wanted to adopt a soldier but he was also heavy in air miles and wanted to know if she had any need for them. Patti had never considered airline miles or had received a request for any, so she told Rich, she'd call him back if anything came up. Less then an half hour later Soldiers Angels got a call from a family whose son had been wounded in Iraq and was now at Walter Reed Hospital in Washington, D.C. for surgery. The Army would fly his wife and child to be with him, but other family members were needed to watch their child while the wife took care of her husband. Then, as if by divine intervention, Patti heard the words, "could Soldiers Angels please provide air fare?" It was almost celestial proof that Patti was put on earth to be a Soldiers Angel. The entire family flew to Washington D.C. that evening on Rich L.'s air miles.

Since that first flight, Soldiers Angels has provided thousands of flights for family members of our wounded heroes. Americans have heard Patti on the radio and thousands have responded by donating thousands of air miles.

"Air miles are so important to our mission. Emergencies arise....Our deployed troops need to get back home immediately because of a death or serious family illness....A spouse or parent of a wounded service member needs to get to the hospital where their loved one has been transported. Unfortunately, they do not always have the resources to pay for an airline ticket. Your donation of air miles will be instrumental in getting our troops and their loved ones together as quickly as possible. You may be asking how it works. ..... You maintain control of the air miles. What we need is your contact information, the number of miles

being donated, the name of the airline and the expiration date, if

any, on the miles. When the need arises, we will contact you to

coordinate getting the airline ticket issued."

Patti Patton Bader during a radio interview

Once the families of our wounded heroes flew to the hospital, they needed a place to stay. Soldiers Angels assessed the families' needs and the needs of the wounded and generously donates to the Fisher House Foundation. The Fisher Houses lodges, feeds, clothes and supports families of the combat wounded for free or at little cost and are located near each of our nation's combat hospitals. Several of the Fisher Houses have awarded Patti Patton Bader and Soldiers Angels numerous Certificates of Appreciation and Awards for Soldiers Angels work, support, contribution and donations to these families. Kathy G., manager of the Landstuhl Germany Fisher House writes, "Working with the Soldiers Angels has been such a help and real joy, for we can give a tangible present to the soldier through his family or directly to say "We all care and we are so proud of the difference you have made in this world, thank you from your supporters".

Eight Air Miles High

Soldiers' Angels makes a difference to the Fisher Houses as well, since the majority of our funding comes from charity, they help us to help the families."

Soldiers Angels believes in the work of the Fisher houses and encourages all Americans to make a monetary contribution to this noble cause.

Dear Soldiers Angels,

I've heard there is a program where I can transfer air miles to soldiers wanting to go home on leave. I have 10,000 miles some-one can have if you write and tell me how to transfer them.

Thanks,

Woodrow M. Sr. Robinson, IL. Vietnam Vet U.S. Army

May No Soldier Go Unloved

Dear Patty:

Our son, Lance Corporal Aaron R., was seriously injured in Iraq on March 18, 2005. The next week you arranged flights for our daughters Hannah (age 10) and Audrey (age 15) to visit Aaron at the National Naval Center. My note is to thank you for your kindness. You and the organization you represent are marvelous. Aaron lost his left leg (below the knee). He is about to go to Walter Reed for Rehabilitation. He is doing great both physically and emotionally. Again, thanks for your help.

May God Bless you,

Randy and Debbie R.

To Soldiers Angels,

Wishing all of you "Happy Holiday" and a "Happy New Year". Thank you for all the wonderful support throughout the years. Especially though, I thank you for helping make the Ft. Campbell Fisher House such a "special" place to be. Unlike the major military treatment facilities, we did not get the kind of support they do. However, you changed that and made possible

Eight Air Miles High

for us to purchase many needed items for the families and items

for the house, which provided much comfort for our families.

You are simply the best and we appreciate you so much.

Best wishes always,

Vivian, FH Families and FH Staff Fort Campbell KY9

Operation Outreach and Operation Top Knot

Operation Outreach was established in November 2003 from a desire to do more to support the wives and children of deployed U.S. soldiers. Deployments are difficult on everyone in the entire family and even more so when the family of the soldier is expecting a child. Patti wanted to commend the women and children at home for their strength, let them know Patti and Soldiers Angels are proud of the sacrifices they make and most importantly to do what can be done to support them during such an emotionally difficult time. Angel Audri C. heads up this successful program.

Patti and Soldiers Angels were receiving many requests from our deployed soldiers not asking for items for themselves, but for their families at home.

When you have a family member in a war zone the worry, stress, struggle and sacrifice is immeasurable. Even in the modern world of satellite cell phones and the internet, it can be weeks or even months between chats before you hear again from a soldier at war. The old saying "No news is good news," is true for those military families stateside. When a soldier's family members go to sleep at night and no one has knocked on their front door; it means that their loved one is most likely still alive and uninjured for another day.

"Soldiers Angels are working to let our heroes know that while they protect us over there, we will help look out for their families here at home." I've overheard Patti say on the phone to several Angels. Some military families have few resources and limited local family assistance.

Operation Outreach provides letters, cards and gifts to these military families especially on their children's birthdays and holidays. Angels in family member's local areas provide military families with "e-pals" or pen pals who know what they're going through; and provide groceries or financial assistance to those families. American troops will tell you, deployment doesn't just affect those who are sent, military families serve too. Additionally, Soldiers Angels Topknot volunteers knit, crochet, sew, quilt and design blankets, booties, hats, bibs and more for the children of deployed soldiers. They also assemble baskets full of goodies such as bottles, diapers, pacifiers, washcloths and grooming kits for the children of our deployed servicemen and women whose families are having trouble "making ends meet."

To the blessed Soldiers Angels:

My husband and I would like to say thank you for all the support and assistance that everyone has provided. Brennan is growing fast and hopefully he'll be out of the hospital in another month. Thank you for being there to aid us into the future. God Bless and Love Always,

The M's Plymouth, IN.

Operation Outreach and Operation Top Knot

Thank you so much for the wonderful baby gifts. The outfit and socks will look great on her also. The baby blanket was beautiful. I can tell it was made with great care and thought.

Sara A.

I just wanted to let everyone know that Adam Ryan was born on 13 OCT 06, 8lbs 13 oz, 20.5 in. A healthy baby boy. I have attached a picture. I want to say thanks for the packages my wife has received. Please continue to support other mothers that are expecting. Once again thank you.

William M.

Dear Friends- Thank you so much for your kindness and thoughtfulness. Receiving your baby care package in the mail was such a surprise. It brought a tear to my eye, and a smile to my face to know that such an extraordinary group of crafters is thinking of our troops and their families. Thanks for your continued support. Keep up the good work!

Amy and Baby Cort

Thank you so much for the wonderful gifts you sent Gabriella. It made me feel so good. It is hard to have a baby alone during the holidays. I included a picture of Gabby with her diaper bag we received. I love it and get tons of compliments about the bag.

Nicole

Thank you so much for the lovely package you sent on behalf of Operation Top Knot. It was so thoughtful! Baby Drew loves the soft blanket and bear, and the outfit was adorable. I really appreciate the coupons. Most of all it is so nice to know there is someone out there supporting our military families. Thanks again to all your contributors.

Kelly A.

Soldier for Kids - Wings of Hope

Dear Lisa,

I am and will be always grateful for your help with our family.

Today we received news that our Jessica will be transported

back to her home area in Ft. Hood and released from the Brooks

Army Medical Center here in San Antonio. There is no doubt in

our minds that having family near by has improved her speedy

recovery. Your help and kind words helped ease the stress and

worries making such a "hurried" trip. Please send our Thanks

and Love to all those who help make this program possible. Our

little Mother will be okay, her 3 week old baby is doing well.

And this ol' grey haired girl sure fell in love with everyone here.

Not to mention. I remember now all the work it takes to care for

an infant. Wow.

Again.. God Bless you and The "Angels"

Laura P., Pittsburgh, PA.

10

Soldiers for Kids – Wings of Hope

Surprisingly most requests came from our deployed soldiers not requesting things for themselves but for other people; wounded comrades, neglected soldiers….and the "locals." There are countless stories of our soldiers helping the people of Iraq and Afghanistan and going out of their way to help those less fortunate.

It's the American way of life; establishing democracy, re-building schools, providing medical aid, and so much more…but it is the children that most dearly have the soldier's hearts. Many of our soldiers go especially above and beyond the call of duty to help the children they come in contact with every day.

Soldier for Kids-Wings of Hope

Children in war-torn areas have so little and have been through so much. They desperately need food, clothing, school supplies, personal hygiene items and an occasional toy or treat can put a huge smile on a child's face! By reaching out and helping to meet some of their needs, our soldiers establish good relationships with the people they're living near and working with -- developing friendship, trust and intelligence sources that help keep them safe and secure.

"Wings of Hope" is a program started when an Airman stationed in Afghanistan contacted Soldiers Angels for help. His unit was working to provide school supplies and other items to Afghani children and their families:

"I have started a little program here for local schools and children/families that do not have much. I have traveled the base asking for the units to donate what ever they can spare as to school supplies and things they think kids would want. I am mostly focusing on school supplies and etc, but there isn't much here for us to get a hold of to give to them" Airman Phillip B.

May No Soldier Go Unloved

When Airman B. e-mailed his Soldiers' Angel for some help and Patti heard about the need, she dubbed the program "Wings of Hope" and started collecting donations for this great cause.

Over the years we have had many requests from our soldiers asking for items to help them in their humanitarian missions to assist local towns and villages and especially the kids. Many of these soldiers are parents or have little brothers and sisters, and their hearts especially go out to these impoverished children. Soldiers often give up their own goodies and snacks to be able to share with the children they see every day.

After we sent a Chaplain Captain hundreds of children's shoes he requested, he sent us pictures of the troops handing them out to poor Afghani children who literally had none and whose feet were black and calloused from months of abuse. The pictures we have received from our troops handing out supplies to the local kids that Soldiers Angels has donated is truly moving and I've put these pictures in a special scrapbook. They always bring a big smile to the viewer.

Soldier for Kids-Wings of Hope

To Bethany Lutheran Church (Soldiers Angels), The Soliders,

Sailors, Airmen, and Marines of Task Force Phoenix V,

made up from 37 states and territories and Puerto Rico

and the 41st Brigade Combat Team of the Oregon National

Guard thank you so very much for your donation for the children

of this proud nation of Afghanistan. You donation proves that the

children of Afghanistan have not been forgotten. Your help goes

a long way to help those who cannot help themselves. Thank you

for the care package.

Take care,

LCDR Tracy R. CJTF Phoenix V Civil Military Operations

Camp Phoenix

PS Photo by 1Lt Catherine F. TF Phoenix - Soldier flying kite

with children of Kabul at the mausoleum of King Nadir Shah.

May No Soldier Go Unloved

Dear Ying and Steve,

Just wanted to drop a quick note to truly thank you for your dedicated support. We have been putting together a baseball team of Iraqi children. We are in the process of acquiring the materials (gloves, bats, etc.) It's great! The kids love it!! Hope all is well. I absolutely loved the B-day pkgs.

Take care-

Amy T. 297th MI BN

Soldier for Kids - Wings of Hope

January 13, 2007

Patti Bader
1792 E. Washington Blvd
Pasadena, CA 91104

Dear Ms. Bader,

My name is LTC Robert Church. I am a JAG officer in the Utah Army National Guard currently serving in Afghanistan. I'm writing to thank you for your donation of the fleece blankets.

I can't tell you how appreciated the blankets were. We took them to a local school and passed them out. The picture is just a glimpse of how much fun it was to pass out the blankets..

I also want to thank Soldier's Angels for their support of the troops. It means so much to us to know that we're being thought of at home. All the gifts and donations your organization sends are so greatly appreciated.

Again, thank you so much for the blankets.

Respectfully,

Robert Church
LTC, JA

http://jagman-tfphoenix.blogspot.com

P.S. Thank you for the boxes of coffee mugs & coffee that you recently sent. They were a huge hit.

Bob

180

11

First Response: Back Packs and Blankets of Hope

Brandon was on patrol in a Humvee near Ar Ramadi, Iraq one cold December morning in 2003, when an Intermediary Explosive Device (IED) went off approximately twenty yards in front of his truck. Brandon's unit had been feeding a local dog. The hound, running ahead of the convoy, accidentally tripped the IED and thankfully saved our son's life.

Brandon remembers flames enveloping him and bits of shrapnel dangerously buzzing around his head. Even though Brandon was within the device's "kill zone," somehow he was unharmed. That couldn't be said for some of his buddies. Several were seriously wounded.

First Response: Back Packs and Blanckets of Hope

The most seriously injured were picked up by Medivac helicopters and rushed to a field hospital in the desert where they were stabilized and then sent on to Landstuhl Regional Medical Center in Germany for immediate surgery. Their clothes had been ripped off and they were strapped to a gurney bed waiting for their operations. They of course hadn't expected to take this life-saving flight and didn't have time to go back and get their stuff, so they woke up coming out of surgery wearing only cool, drafty, hand-me-down backless white hospital gowns.

When Patti found out this had happened to one of Brandon's friends, Specialist Brian M., she decided to stock Landstuhl Regional Medical Center with "First Response Back Packs" and "Blankets of Hope." Patti called her father for help and he in turn enlisted the assistance of his fellow Westpoint graduates, class of 1955. They raised and donated funds for the first hundred First Response Backpacks.

A First Response Backpack is a backpack stuffed with necessary personal items like a toothbrush, toothpaste, comb, shampoo, soap and articles of clothing and undergarments that a wounded soldier needs upon waking from surgery. A phone card is included so the soldiers can call their family members while they recover.

Patti wanted to add a personal touch to each waking wounded hero to tell them we care. Therefore, each First Response Backpack also contains a "Blanket of Hope" which is *handmade* by a Soldiers' Angels volunteer. In one instance, an Angel named Diane L. found out that because of the need, 12 First Response Backpacks were going out the next day without Blankets of Hope in them. She stayed up all night and sewed the 12 Blankets of Hope by morning and shipped them at her own expense. Doctors, nurses and family members have written to Patti to describe the healing powers that these "Blankets of Hope" have had on their patients and loved ones.

The greatest recognition has come from the wounded heroes themselves. One soldier wrote, "I want to thank your organization personally for the backpacks that you have provided for the wounded and sick soldiers here.... As the 1SG of this company, I want you to know that these backpacks put smiles on the sol-

First Response: Back Packs and Blanckets of Hope

diers' faces and that's priceless." A hospital worker recounted her experience with a soldier who had received a First Response Backpack, saying, "When his parents arrived, the first thing he showed them was his Purple Heart, the second was his Blanket of Hope from Soldiers Angels! I cannot tell you the emotional thank you we received from this young soldier's mother!" In another instance a wounded soldier's mother wrote, "Dear Soldiers' Angels, Thank you for the blanket, my son won't let go of it."

To date Soldiers Angels has provided over 10,000 First Response Backpacks and Blankets of Hope to our military's busiest combat hospital, Landstuhl Regional Medical Center in Germany. The First Response Backpack and Blankets of Hope program have been so successful that Patti is working with the Army to implement the program in all U.S. combat hospitals. In May 2006, the Department of Defense awarded Patti Patton Bader the Civilian Award for Humanitarian Service, the highest award the Department can give to a civilian.

May No Soldier Go Unloved

"For exceptional dedication and selfless service leading to the creation of the <u>Soldiers Angels Foundation</u> which has immeasurably enriched the lives of countless thousands of service members and their families. Ms. Patton-Bader's talent and marketing skills provided them a myriad of services and unending support at this critical time in our nations fight to end global terrorism. Her selfless service, abundant generosity and tireless care reflect great credit on her, the American Soldier and the United States Of America."

Lt.General Kevin C. Kiley MC Commanding

Dear Patti,

My name is SSG Scotty C. and I just wanted to send you my Thanks for your comforting items given to me during my recovery in Iraq on your behalf. If it wasn't for your gift I wouldn't have had any items. I thank you and everyone involved. It definitely put a smile on my face. Thanks again.

Your friend,

Scott E. C. C 168 AR BN

First Response: Back Packs and Blanckets of Hope

To all the Soldiers Angels,

On behalf of all the doctors, nurses, corpsman, and Marines at Al Asad's Surgical Company in Iraq, thank you so much for all the great backpacks! My name is Donna S. and I'm a LT in the Navy Nurse Corps stationed with the Marines at Al Asad. I can't begin to describe how good it feels to hand out those goody-filled backpacks to my patients – the wounded and ill marines, Soldiers, and Sailors that come into our hospital. To date, we have seen over 420 patients since our company took over in February. Our patients have a wide variety of illnesses and injuries, ranging from minor to life-threatening. Several have given the ultimate sacrifice. When a trauma patient comes in, they are usually flown in, with no time to stop and pack a bag. We cut all their clothes off to expose the injuries and treat them. These patients are the ones we give out the "soldiers angels" backpacks to. They are perfect! The patients have enough supplies in those bags for at least 5 days, which gives them time to heal and recover. We love the backpacks and giving them to our troops is a most rewarding experience. Thank you so much for supplying them to us. I don't know if the guys who are getting the back-

packs are writing to you...some of them may be too tired or hurt.

But I can personally assure you that they are being used and ap-

preciated! Thanks so much!!

Sincerely,

Donna K. S. LT, NC, USA

And thanks from the entire company A Surgical Co. Al Asad,

Iraq

Dear Ms. Patton-Bader,

My name is Jeani F. and I am a psychiatric nurse currently de-

ployed to Southwest Asia. I work in a facility that ensures ill and

injured troops are flown out of the country to a hospital better

equipped to their needs. Many times these brave men and women

come to our facility without personal items due to their particu-

lar circumstances. Today we received 14 boxes from Soldiers

Angels each containing 3 backpacks. Each backpack had per-

sonal care items, a small handmade quilt, socks, and other

First Response: Back Packs and Blanckets of Hope

clothing items. It has been an honor for me to make sure these backpacks are given to sick and wounded troops. I don't have the words to describe to you the feeling I get seeing the incredulous look on their faces when they realize these are gifts from their countrymen. It is most definitely tear producing! The thank you card you filled out was also packed in the box. I try to personally contact anyone who has provided their name and address. Every card we receive makes it way to the pillow of a troop. I have seen battle weary individuals wipe their eyes as they read the warm wishes and prayers. The short amount of time it took you to write encouraging words on the card has made an immeasurable impact on a particular soldier/airman/sailor's life. They aren't always in a position to write their thanks while they are with us so I want to do one more thing for these young men and women......

Thank you for your support.

Jeani F.

Capt USAF NC

A special thank you for the wonderful work you are doing with

May No Soldier Go Unloved

Soldiers Angels. As a mother, wife, sister, and soldier, I appreci-

ate the efforts you are making to help America's young men and

women during difficult and trying time in their lives.

Dear Soldiers Angels,

We received the back packs you sent to Chief F. a couple of

days ago and they are wonderful. I must admit when the Chief

first approached me I was apprehensive but after seeing them I

can not thank you enough, they are exactly what we need. One

backpack with everything the wounded soldier needs. Our mis-

sion in the CASF is to temporarily hold and transport all the

wounded in Iraq out to Germany. We process about 30 a day but

not all have a need for your backpack, we estimated about 3-5 a

day come with nothing. Thanks in advance for any help you can

provide.

Mike B. Col, USAF Commander Expeditionary Aerospace

Medicine Squadron Balad

First Response: Back Packs and Blanckets of Hope

Dear Soldiers' Angels,

I really appreciate the boxes of backpacks that you sent for our soldiers in the ward. They (patients/troopers) were very happy to know that there are people that really care about their welfare. The smiles that were on their faces were priceless. As the 1SG of this Troop Medical Clinic (TMC), I really appreciate this from the bottom of my hearts. You have a first class organization when it comes to taking care of troops. Thanks in advance for everything. I would also like to wish you and your staff a Happy Holidays.

Take care and God Bless,

1SG Jimmie

Dear Patti Bader,

You do not know me but my name is Venina W. and I received the Soldier's Angels package while I was in the hospital in Kuwait. I am 27 years old and I am originally from Jacksonville, Florida. I am currently deployed in Iraq. While in Iraq, I was wounded and was taken by aircraft to Kuwait for treatment. Un-

fortunately, I was not able to bring any items with me. At my stay in the hospital, a nurse gave me a backpack filled with numerous items inside. In the bottom of the backpack was a slip saying this package was sent by Soldiers Angels and that is why I am writing this letter. I want to personally thank everyone involved with Soldiers Angels and also for your time and generous gift. These items in the backpack were very well needed and appreciated. I work as a medic in a clinic and understand how to take care of a soldiers' physical and mental wellbeing. This package gave me a warm feeling in my heart knowing that people care and will take the time out to help and support us.

Once Again Sincerely

Venina W. CCO 325 B5B/25 ID,

First Response: Back Packs and Blanckets of Hope

Dear Soldiers Angels,

This kind of support usually comes from family, not home front strangers who have hearts of gold. There are not enough thank yous to give to you all. You are absolutely wonderful. Your care packs are just in time for our mission of _____. We are taking them with us in our ambulances.

SSG D.

Dear Cathy,

My son Matthew is a patient in the ICU and was the recipient of a blanket of hope in his room. Although he is on a ventilator, what a wonderful gift to drape over him; to give him a sense of warmth and loving kindness. Such acts of kindness are appreciated from me his dad who flew in from Florida to be at his bedside. Thank you so much from my heart,

Ivan Q.

May No Soldier Go Unloved

Dear Soldiers Angels,

I wanted you to know what ya'll are doing for these soldiers.

They travel with their blankets from here, hopefully all the way

home.

:) Lori C

Patti,

My husband came home from work the other day and said, "Hey

my boss says thank you for the

backpack." Since his boss is in St. Louis I didn't have a clue

what he was talking about. He says, "You know those Soldiers

Angels ones!" His boss's nephew was wounded in Iraq and got

shipped to Germany with exactly what he had on. Minus what

clothing was cut off to work on him. (He had a major arm in-

jury) This soldier said that backpack was a Godsend!!! He had

never appreciated anything so much. Just thought I would share

that you are touching people that are closer than you think!!!

Elaine

First Response: Back Packs and Blanckets of Hope

Dear Maryann,

I am an ICU nurse at the 10th Combat Support Hospital and I just wanted to thank Soldiers' Angels for the wonderful blankets! This is a great program and I know it takes a lot of work to make all of the blankets but they are truly appreciated. We make sure all of our patients leave the ICU for Germany wrapped up in one of these special blankets from home.

More often than not the guys we take care of are critically ill and are on ventilators but I hope that these blankets make it through the journey home with them.

The blankets always bring a smile to the ICU staff member faces as well as the faces of the wounded soldier, and comrades who often come to visit their buddies before they air evac out of theater.

It is nice to see that they are not forgotten and it is an excellent token of appreciation! Thanks again your group is truly inspiring!

Sincerely,

Erin I. 10th CSH-ICU

May No Soldier Go Unloved

Hi Sue,

I am writing to say thank you! Your beautiful eagle blanket made it's way around my fiancé's shoulders! On the sixteenth of this month, his vehicle ran over a land mine. Rodney's injuries were mainly to his face. He was taken to Germany, without even a shirt on, as the doctors had cut it off him. Someone, somewhere, along the way, gave him your blanket. He said it was the warmest blanket ever given to him! So, from the bottom of my heart, I say THANK YOU! May God bless you for the time and effort you put into that blanket!

Vicky

Dear Patti,

Our Blankets Really Make a Difference......Oh Yes They Do!!!

My sister in Waynesboro, Virginia was having her garage sale today and one of her sons friends from high school was there. She asked him how he was doing and he told her he was in the Marines.

Well.......she has been helping me, trying to get blankets made to

First Response: Back Packs and Blanckets of Hope

send to the Combat Support Hospitals (CSH), in Germany and Fort Campbell Kentucky, for Beth and her team....My sister told him about Soldiers Angels and a presentation she did at her church trying to get some sewers interested in helping with our project. She told him about her slide presentation showing a transport plane carrying the wounded soldiers out of Iraq.

You are not going to believe it!.........he said "I was on one of those planes" and this is what made the hair stand up on her arms and mine too when she told me about it.......he said he was naked, laying on a gurney and the only thing covering him was ONE OF OUR BLANKETS. He kept the blanket, found the email address of the angel that sent it to him, to thank her personally. Now he has the blanket on his bed, where he says it will stay. If anyone needs a little inspiration.........THIS IS IT! It's just a blanket........but it means so much to a wounded soldier! The patriotic fabric is on sale now, so we can whip up some pretty nice blankets!! Thought I'd share,

Sharon

Heart for the wounded Proud Blankets Of Hope Team member

May No Soldier Go Unloved

Hi Patti,

I wanted to pass this on to you about Jeff, the injured Marine. He was sent to Germany, then to a hospital in Maryland for further repair and rehab. His folks were flown to Maryland last Wednesday and returned Sunday. At work the next day, his Mom told me Jeff had his BLANKET with him! She said that it was practically the only thing he had with him when he arrived in Maryland. THANK YOU SO MUCH!!!!!!!!! God Bless you for making sure he got one of your blankets. You're a blessing to those soldiers and for that I thank you from the bottom of my heart.

Kim

First Response: Back Packs and Blanckets of Hope

Hi Dear Ms B.,

One of your blankets today went to a wounded soldier who lost his friends. It is heartbreaking to listen to him talk about his friends and the incident. The blanket has a special meaning to him, and although he has a long road to recovery, I know he will never let it go. Your display of compassion and patriotism means so much to them. It was indeed an honor to pass on the blanket to this soldier who placed everything on the line to protect our freedom.

MAJ C. M., 10th CSH (Combat Support Hospital)

Mrs. Bader,

If it had not been for your support I would have had nothing. I know that a blanket may not seem like much back home, but here it can make a lot of difference. You will never know how much you helped me.

SGT John M.

May No Soldier Go Unloved

Hi,

I was recently wounded in combat in Iraq..It was a pretty good hit and when I was medevac'd obviously I didn't get to grab some important items:) I woke up the next day and had nothing to wear or any hygiene stuff..my uniform I had on was blood-soaked and unwearable..This very sweet nurse (in the pic) brought me a backpack full of goodies from you folks and there was even pajamas:) the hospital robes didn't fit me and I just managed to squeeze your clothes on:) I felt a lot better with a shower and some pants on...all with your gift. I ended up having to go to a few more hospitals by helicopter to get some specialist work done as some of the wounds were deep..I took the bag with me everywhere it was all I had..It was the best thing that could have happened at that time..I just wanted to say thank you for all you nice people do...Here is a pic when I was released...my nurse, my friend on the left and that's me with the new "face job".

Thanks again,

Sgt. C. 1461 combat het/gun truck plt.

First Response: Back Packs and Blanckets of Hope

Ms. Bader and fellow contributors with the "Soldiers Angels"-

I would like to extend heartfelt thanks for all the staff here at TQ

Surgical, Iraq. Your boxes of "goodies" - sweats, etc. could not

have come at a better time. Although we have a terrific supply

system here – mass casualties are trained for, but not expected.

When they occur – they clean us out. Your generous goods ar-

rived just in time to ensure and assist us in providing the troops

the very best! We thank you for your time and effort to coordi-

nate this support effort. Know that we are so very thankful for

the exceptional Americans and patriots such as yourselves!

God Bless and Keep You,

Julie B. CDR/NC/USN Sr. Nurse TQ Surgical Iraq

Hello,

I recently received a backpack that you had prepared for

wounded soldiers. I often get asked "do you need anything" or

"what can I send?" I always reply nothing because I make an

okay amount of money and I can afford little things such as

toothpaste and underwear. I was unfortunate enough to be sent

May No Soldier Go Unloved

to Kuwait after a minor surgery with nothing but a set of combat uniforms and a physical fitness uniform. I had no toiletries or anything because my unit had to gather what they could and cram it into a backpack on short notice while I was in a hospital bed recovering. The items in the backpack that I received when I made it to Kuwait for recovery helped me out a lot and it was the little things such as toiletries that I had turned down before. I appreciate what you do along with hundreds of other soldiers who daily go through the same routine as I did. Thanks so much and may GOD bless you and your families.

PFC Donald W. H. MP | 128 MP CO Alabama Army National Guard

First Response: Back Packs and Blanckets of Hope

Dear Ms. Patton Bader:

The women of St. James Episcopal Church in Pewee Valley, Kentucky make "Healing Blankets" approx. three feet square which we give to people who are ill or request them for sick friends etc. These blankets are blessed by our priest, Rev. Paul J. and have a prayer enclosed with them. We would very much like to send you some of these blankets if you feel you would like to put them in back packs. Please let me know if this plan is acceptable and I will ship some to you in the near future.

Yours sincerely,

Mary B.

12

Wounded Warriors

Soldiers that are severely injured, especially amputees and burn victims, sometimes need months and even years of therapy to heal. The Army flies these wounded soldiers from a major combat hospital, like Walter Reed in Washington D.C., to other Army hospitals, either near their families, or to a hospital that specializes in the care they need. Because of the number of Soldiers Angels across the country, no matter where a wounded soldier is sent, there are always a couple of Angels who live nearby who can visit.

In 2003, Patti contacted Lieutenant Colonel James R. at Brook Army Medical Center (BAMC) in San Antonio, TX to check on a couple of wounded soldiers the Angels had adopted. For political reasons, nobody in the Army can ask for assistance from civilians or call a press conference to tell us they need help. The Army is supposed to be self-sufficient. "I know you can't ask me for stuff," Patti told Lt. Colonel James R., "and this phone call never occurred. But theoretically, if by chance, these things arrived at your hospital without your knowledge, which of them would you need the most: clothes, phone cards, food, or gift cards? I want to know what you really need, or else, I could end up sending you a bunch of stuff you can't use." "They all sound good to me," he replied, "and it is always nice to give out phone cards."

It was the start of a great team. Patti and Lt. Colonel James R. have developed a good working relationship together over the years. When Lt. James R. recently retired after his distinguished career in the service, he joined Soldiers Angels as a board member and advisor and is now head of all the Soldiers Angels Wounded Warrior Projects.

Visiting the wounded at the hospitals can be a very emotionally sobering experience and isn't for everyone. What always amazes me about the military wounded is the lack of self pity they all seem to have for themselves. Some of these heroes actually feel guilty about getting wounded and leaving their comrades behind in the battlefield. Hundreds of times, the Angels have offered a wounded soldier recovering in a hospital bed "anything he wanted or needs" and the soldier would ask for something for his wife, mother, child, or fellow soldier instead. Some of these heroes are blind, without limbs, or severely burned; and their first concern is not for themselves, but for their loved ones.

Wounded hero SPC. Steve A., a double amputee, just wanted some gold hoop earrings for his wife at Christmas. SGT Mike M. recovering from brain surgery, only wanted a string of pearls for his wife's birthday. Private Gabe G., recovering for months

Wounded Warriors

from severe burn injuries, didn't want anything for himself. Instead, he asked if Soldiers Angels could do something special for his mother, who had sat at his bedside 24/7 during his recovery. A mother of a wounded soldier with very limited means who was asked what she needed, requested an "easy chair" so her wounded son could sit more comfortably. The wooden chairs she had were old and she couldn't afford to buy new ones. These selfless acts I've seen from wounded soldiers and military families have been truly inspirational and dramatically changed my perception of life. Most of my day-to-day worries seem pretty meaningless in comparison.

May No Soldier Go Unloved

Dear Soldiers Angels,

First of all, we would like to give a very heartfelt "Thank You"

to each and every one of you. Each one of you has sent a card or

a letter to us this year. We wish you could know the impact it has

had on us. These wonderful cards and letters came from all over

the United States and were filled with well wishes, promises of

prayer, wonderful stories of how you live, phone cards, pictures,

invitations to visit, and each one was from the heart. Some, we

were able to answer. Then as the cards continued pouring in, it

became difficult to respond to each one, We want you to know

that we are so grateful for each and every one of you. This is

such a wonderful ministry. If you are still receiving names from

Soldiers Angels, please don't stop writing. For a soldier lying in

a hospital bed, each day at mail call become a very special time.

Wayne was stationed near Baghdad with his Army National

Guard Unit. On January 27 of this year, I received notice that he

was in the hospital in Germany awaiting brain surgery. I got to

Germany hours before surgery. The object was lodged 3 inches

deep and it was a miracle that he was still alive. As a result of

surgery, many blood vessels were ruptured and things were dis-
located inside his head. He was left with memory loss. But God
is good. Everything is slowly healing and going back into place
and his memory is continuing to get better. We were told that the
healing process could take up to two years. Although we have
been through many tough situations this year, we have been so
blessed and seen so many miracles. We both have a new per-
spective on life now. Praise God! When we first arrived at
Walter Reed Hospital in Washington D.C., a representative from
Soldiers Angels met with us. She told us that no wish was too big
or too small to be granted. As we talked, she discovered that mu-
sic has always played a big part in Wayne's life. She saw to it
that he was given a guitar to keep. With his memory loss, it was
such a thrill to hear him play a song all the way through! That
guitar was wonderful in the healing process. Thank you Soldiers
Angels! Now we are finally home again and things are returning
to normal. We spent much of the year in military and veterans
hospitals. I tried to take a leave of absence from work an am
thrilled to be back. Wayne is being medically retired from the

Army. He is working at the Armory for the time being, awaiting final paperwork that releases him permanently. The rest of his unit returned home in time for Thanksgiving.

Precious Soldiers Angels, we want you to realize how much you are appreciated. The small act of sending a card or letter means more then you'll ever know. Thank you from the bottom of our hearts!

Wayne and Terri M., Madisonville, TN

Patti,

Hope this got to you in time. My American Soldier hero is Dean P., SSG U.S. Army, ret. Soon after becoming part of the (Soldiers Angels) Wounded TLC team, I was given his name as not only a wounded soldier, but also as a fellow angel. His thank you to my card and letter was very moving. My card and letter was the first he had received. He wrote "Thank you just doesn't seem to justify what I feel in my heart. I don't know if I could express it in words." I keep the thank you card where I can see it everyday and it is my inspiration to keep helping our wounded

Wounded Warriors

heroes. SSG P. was wounded in the first days of Iraqi Freedom and he has since been an integral part of Soldiers Angels. In the Army he was a tank crewman and for the last 12 years was a weapons specialist in the Rangers. He lived being a Ranger. I am proud of his life with me because he has motivated me to be the best Angel on the Wounded TLC team that I can be. He truly represents the spirit of our wounded American heroes. His dedication and sacrifice needs to be honored and remembered forever.

Sincerely,

Amy D. Muskegan, MI.

May No Soldier Go Unloved

Dear Fay,

We would like to let you know just how much we appreciate your love and support. We have received thousands of phone calls, emails, and letters from all over the world. Your prayers have sustained us and truly helped Chris though this trying time. Everyday he gets a little stronger and hopefully soon he will be released from Loma Linda Medical Center making a full recovery and able to join his battalion at 29 Palms California. So many of you have offered to help in so many different ways and we are grateful to each and every one of you. We are especially grateful to the Family of Laralee B., who gave Chris the Gift of Life through their kind act of Organ Donation. We will never be able to thank you enough! Many of you asked if there is anything you can do for Chris and our family. The answer is YES! Please continue to Pray for his full recovery and if you are not already signed up to be an Organ Donor, please consider doing so. You may someday save the life of someone just like Chris waiting for the GIFT OF LIFE. Fay, thanks so much for the card – the words of encouragement really help. We appreciate the work you do with Soldiers Angels, it is so important to keep letting the guys know just how great they truly are! Keep up the good work you are doing – God Bless,

Susan L. Proud Marine Mom of LCpl Chris L.

Dear Soldiers Angels,

What a wonderful ministry you have to America's Soldiers. My husband Wayne, was a patient at Walter Reed Hospital when your organization loaned him a guitar. What a surprise when one day at Richmond VA Hospital, he received a guitar to keep for his own. He has had brain surgery and as a result, has short term memory loss. He has always loved the guitar, and for him to pick it up and remember a song from beginning to end, was some of the best medicine he received. Thank you for the wonderful gift. Every time he picks up his guitar, we are reminded of your generosity.

May No Soldier Go Unloved

Dear Ying and Steve,

This is Benjamin L. T., the soldier you have written to from Soldiers Angels. I wanted to personally thank you for taking the time to write me and expressing your concern for my injury. I realize it takes a lot of time to request a soldier to write to and I really appreciate your support. To give you a little idea where I came from, I'm a 24 year old from Round Rock, Texas (just north of Austin). I joined the Army when I was 20 years old, just as the Invasion of Iraq was first kicking off. Right out of basic training I was sent to Korea for what was supposed to be one year tour of duty. I actually took a lot of pride getting to go there and being a third generation of T's to serve the country. After being in Korea 11 months, my unit (the 2ⁿᵈ Brigade of the 2ⁿᵈ Infantry Division) was alerted that some of our battalions would be getting deployed to Iraq.

Because we were an infantry unit, members of my company expected that our company would be selected to go. However, it turned out that my company wasn't selected at all. I felt that it was an important mission so when they requested volunteers to

Wounded Warriors

fill in for soldiers who wouldn't be able to be deployed I volun-

teered to join Charlie Company and deploy to Iraq. About three

months after my friends and I left my old company to joined

Charlie Company, we were off to Kuwait. We spent 3 weeks

there getting acclimated to the desert weather and training up

on mostly urban fighting before we left to our next duty station

which was Camp Junction, in Ramadi. Ramadi really isn't too

bad and some things were actually fun. Most of our days there

were spent patrolling highways and performing a mission called

IED denial. In non Army terms it pretty much meant we were

supposed to find road side before they found our convoys.

Another mission we were on a good bit of the time was QRF, or

quick reaction force. That pretty much meant if someone got into

a fight, or was hit by a road side bomb, and needed assistance

we would rush out there as fast as we could in our HMMVYs and

Bradleys and try to help out.

And last, but certainly not least, were raids. They were never

boring and always kept you on your toes. Some times we'd go

raid suspected houses for 8 hours and find nothing, and yet other times we'd find some real bad guys in the first house we'd

raid on a mission. On one of the raids we busted one guy who we

believe was involved in the beheading which were taking place

at that time. My team was actually awarded a R&R trip back to

Kuwait as a result of busting that bad guy, but I was hurt before

I could go on that trip. After being in Ramadi about 4 month my

company was selected to lead a Marine assault into the city of

Fallujah. At that time Fallujah was full of insurgents and we had

absolutely no military presence in the city. Before the battle

started an estimated 1,000 insurgents in the city swore they

would rather die then give back their haven to U.S. and Iraqi

forces. We started the Fallujah operation just after midnight on

a Monday morning. We went in with the objective of taking con-

trol of the hospital which was on the west side of Fallujah. This

hospital had been used by the bad guys for PR purposes during

a previous Fallujah operation. When we went into the area the

bad guys were indeed using the hospital as a position of fire and

had to be forcefully removed. After the hospital was secure we

repositioned to a nearby abandoned police building where we remained for the next few days. Four days into the battle my company still hadn't been resupplied and we were very low on everything from food, water, and even bullets. When our resupply convoy got ambushed for the third time we were forced to take my platoon out to help them. We arrived at the ambush site about 3:00 AM and set up a defensive position for security for the convoy. Shortly after we were in position, the insurgents that originally ambushed the convoy set off another IED and started up on us with small arms fire from in front of us and from our side. It only took about 30 seconds from when the IED went off until the last shots were fired, but when it was all over I had been shot in the leg and two insurgents had been killed by our small arms fire. Once it all calmed down I had been patched up by our medic and put inside a Bradley, fighting broke back out again. This time it only lasted a couple of seconds before it all stopped. One of our Bradleys, using infrared sights, found a couple of insurgents hiding behind a berm. It wasn't actually much of a fight and none of our guys were hurt this time. From start to end it wasn't even 30 minutes from the time I got shot until a Chinook helicopter dropped me off at a field hospital at Balad and I was in surgery. The bullet hit me in the side of my leg and blew out a lot of my tibia.

After being in Lundstuhl, Germany for three days and another two surgeries I was sent to Andrews Air Force Base, Fort Carson, Colorado, and finally to my new home at Brooke Army Medical Center in San Antonio, Texas. Since arriving there I've had seven more surgeries moving tissue and muscle around in my calf and bone grafts to replace the missing bone. For 14 months I had metal pins sticking out my leg, but now the pins are out of my leg and I'm walking without a cane or crutches. I do walk with a pretty good limp now, but I think it will get better. If anything good came out of it, I now have some cool scars and a good story to tell. I'm now in physical therapy just to regain muscle memory which I lost from being down for awhile, but it's nothing I can complain about. It doesn't take you long at BAMC before you see an injury a lot worse than yours to realize it's impossible to feel bad about yourself. Thank you again for you kind words and the time you took to let someone you don't even know feel very appreciated. Only a couple of sentences go a long

way. Thanks again,

Spc. Benjamin L. T.

Dear Soldiers Angels,

I just wanted to write a few lines and say how much your organi-

zation means to me and what you have done for me.

I was deployed to the Mideast for about 9 months and if it

weren't for Soldiers Angels, I don't think I would have made it. I

really did look forward to the letters and hearing from all of you.

And I tried to write everyone that wrote to me. It was my escape

from a really bad environment and it meant so much to me for

you all to take the time to write me, someone that you didn't

even know, and share so much. I felt like I had a family that

really cared about me and how I was doing.

Then, I returned back to the states and because of an injury. I

have been on medical hold here in San Diego waiting to get

fixed so that I can return back home. I have been away from

home for almost 2 years as an activated Navy Reservist. My home is in Oklahoma and I am currently here in San Diego.

Well, I have been going through my own mess here and have had 2 surgeries all alone here and I finally got myself together to send out Christmas cards. I got so many letters and phone calls in return. I was so touched that so many people really care even after we get home.

I just went through my 3rd surgery and I have had so much support from Soldiers Angels that there is no way that I am going to not get well. I had been so depressed before and wanted to just die but you all have really changed that for me. Your organization has changed my life. You all mean so much to me and I hope to be able to do what you do once I leave this place and get back to the real world.

I just wanted to say how important you have been to me and how much your support has meant to me. Thank you so much for everything and thank you for taking your time to care for us and for being there for us.

With much love and appreciation,

Vickie L. MN2, United States Navy, active reserve

13

Operation Valor IT

In June 2005, Patti was notified of an Army Captain who suffered terrible injuries by an IED attack in Iraq. In addition to being a captain, Captain Z. was a blogger who had now lost the use of his hands, in addition to other injuries, in the explosion. Captain Z's wife kept up his blog while he recovered from his wounds at Walter Reed Hospital, so his friends could be informed on his condition.

When Patti learned of his situation, she procured a laptop computer and Captain Z. installed special voice activated software. This software allows those suffering from severe arm, hand, or eye injuries, to use a computer by "speaking" at it. Wounded heroes could surf the web and send and receive email from friends and family.

May No Soldier Go Unloved

The difference in Captain Z's recovery was amazing. He not only re-sumed his blog, but encouraged other handicapped and amputee soldiers to contact Soldiers Angels to receive their own voice activated software and laptops. "At that time I had no use of either hand. I know how humbling it is, how humiliating it feels. And I know how much better I felt - how amazingly more functional I felt - after Soldiers' Angels provided me with a laptop and a loyal reader provided me with the software. I can't wait to do the same, to give that feeling to another soldier at Walter Reed."

These events inspired Captian Z. to ask Patti to provide a library of voice activated laptops to our military hospitals for handicapped heroes to use while recovering from their wounds. Patti put the word out on her website and the military bloggers started a contest to see which branch of the service could raise the most funds for this project. They not only raised enough donations to equip the hospitals with laptops, but enough to actually give the laptops as permanent gifts to several thousand of these wounded heroes to date. A former World War II physician, Doctor T. has personally donated over six figures in monetary contributions over the last year to help support Operation Valor IT. I am truly amazed and thankful for his generosity.

In September 2006, the Military Order of Purple Hearts awarded Patti Patton Bader with the George Washington Spirit Award for Soldiers Angels contribution to the combat wounded, which is the highest honor bestowed by the Order to a non-member.

Dear Patti,

Thank you very much for the check and voice activated lap top. It will be a big step in Adams' ongoing recovery and will greatly empower him in so many ways. God Bless!

Thank You, Nancy S.

P.S. We will be at the Mologne House while Adam continues to do out-patient at Walter Reed in Washington. Hopefully in six months we will be able to return home to Minnesota. Thank you again from a grateful mother!!

May No Soldier Go Unloved

Dear Mrs. Bader,

Thank you for supporting our wounded Marines and Sailors. Your donations are heartfelt and deeply appreciated. Mere words cannot describe the lasting impact you are making in the lives of those returning. Words of your generosity are reaching far, as the wounded share the good news with the families across the country.

Very Sincerely Thank You.

The Service Members of Operation Iraqi Freedom.

Commanding General, Office of the Division Inspectors`, 1st

Marine Division, Camp Pendleton, CA.

Dear Lynette, Anthony, Neil

Thank you all so much for coming to see me yesterday. It's always nice to meet new people and see their support for me and my fellow servicemen and women. Thank you so much for providing me with the laptop. It will help me greatly during my hospital stay and lengthy rehab. Good luck to you Neil as you continue to heal from your wound. Thanks for coming to the hospital to encourage me and my family.

Operation Valor IT

God Bless and Thank you all again,

Sgt. Andrew R. and family Wrightstown, N.J.

Dear Patti,

I wanted to write you in regards to my lap-top, software and case. Thank You! I wish I could say or do more. The laptop and voice activated software is allowing me to return to college. My limited vision/vision loss has limited me to writing very little, but I wanted to write to you personally. I'm very grateful for all the cards and letters I've received from all the Soldiers Angels around the country. I have responded to each of them. The wounded warriors barracks has been very instrumental in my recovery. I'm also grateful for all they too have done.

Yours truly,

HM (FMF) Glenn "Doc" M. Clarksburg, Ohio

May No Soldier Go Unloved

Soldiers Angels

I was not aware of your organization until this past weekend when I learned that you presented my nephew with a new laptop computer. My nephew is 1LT Ferris B. and he is being treated at Walter Reed Medical Center for injuries sustained in Iraq just before Christmas. He is expected to undergo numerous surgeries, skin grafts, and a long recovery period so the laptop computer will be very important to him. Ferris and his entire family are grateful for your organization's generosity.

I have enclosed a small contribution as a token of my appreciation for all that you do.

With sincere gratitude,

James M. B. LTC (Ret) US Army

Certificates and Awards

DEPARTMENT OF THE ARMY
C Company, Task Force 1-7
Forward Operating Base Summerall
Bayji, Iraq
APO, AE 09392

AETV-BG-AT-B-C

December 28, 2004

Dear Friends of the Soldiers of Charlie Company,

I want to thank you on behalf of the soldiers of C Company, Task Force 1-7 for the care packages you sent. We have appreciated the support you have shown over the past 10 ½ months of our deployment. We are now preparing to head back to Germany and finally be reunited with our friends and family there. Our soldiers have fought hard and have also been part of the reconstruction efforts here. Hopefully our efforts to affect individual people in town will help change this country and the people of Iraq will get to experience the freedom that we know in America.

If you still wish to support some of the troops that will be residing on our FOB, you can send them care packages at the following address:

XO, A/1-111 IN, TF 1/103rd
FOB Summerall, OIF III
APO, AE 09393

Again, we have appreciated the support over the past year. We will appreciate your prayers and thoughts as we move into the final stage of our deployment.

Sincerely,

James K. Starling
First Lieutenant, U.S. Army
Executive Officer

May No Soldier Go Unloved

DEPARTMENT OF THE ARMY
COMBINED/JOINT TASK FORCE (CJTF-76)
TASK FORCE THOROUGHBRED
BAGRAM, AFGANISTHAN
APO AE 09354

To Whom It May Concern:

The combined forces of Army, Navy, Air Force, and Marines stationed at Bagram Air Field, Afghanistan would like to express their sincere gratitude for your humanitarian donation. Although the service men and women are here on a military mission your contributions made it possible for them to make a difference to the people of Afghanistan in a very personal and memorable way.

Many of the people in this region suffer from mal-nutrition. They barely have enough resources to buy food for their families. As a result children are often undersize. A child looking to be 10 years old may actually be in their early to mid teen years. Proper clothing is scarce to say the least. Children are often without shoe's or warm clothing for the winter months. The terrain here is very rough and rocky, and the weather can be harsh in summer or winter. The clothing received by the Afghan people is a huge blessing.

The combined forces here were blessed to be able to help in a more personal way than their military missions would have allowed. Distributing the humanitarian items put the soldiers and airmen in direct contact with the innocent people we are here to support. Our continuing aid is the best way to strengthen our relationship to the Afghan people. Thanks again for your Generosity.

SSG Jeff Dierk
Chaplain Assistant
Task Force Thoroughbred

P.S. What we most need now is clothing and shoes.

DEPARTMENT OF THE ARMY
6TH TRANSPORTATION BATTALION (TRUCK)
CAMP ARIFJAN, KUWAIT
APO, AE 09366

January 2, 2005

Office of the Adjutant

Dear Supporters,

On behalf of the commander, 6th Transportation Battalion I wanted to express our appreciation for all the support we have received from individuals like you since our deployment here in September. I am proud to let you know that the soldiers were able to have a Christmas party on 21 December and it would not have been possible without your generous care packages.

I wanted to mention some of the thoughtful and useful items that we have received that we would have never thought of:

Christmas cards, trees, and decorations, golf clubs, hand knitted slippers, Halloween candy, cards for all special occasions, subscriptions to magazines, DVD's of television shows, and calendars.

Our truck drivers have a new year of missions ahead of them with many units rotating back to the area and others rotating back to the states. They will be driving hundreds of thousands of miles and moving thousands of tons of equipment. Your support has brought a little piece of home to soldiers in a land far from home. I wish you the best in this new year.

Sincerely,

Jesse R. Wentworth
Captain, US Army
Adjutant

Dear Patti,

Thank you especially for the nice note and sharing our unit's name with the angels! We wish you the best this new year.

Jesse

May No Soldier Go Unloved

DEPARTMENT OF THE ARMY
293rd Military Police Company
LSA Diamondback (Al Mosul, Iraq)
Army Post Office AE 09334

January 15, 2005

Soldiers' Angels
1792 E. Washington Blvd
Pasadena, CA 911044

Dear Soldiers' Angels, Bernina Sewing Groups and the Pigon Family and Friends,

I would like to thank everyone at Soldiers' Angels, Bernina Sewing Groups and the Pigons Family and Friends for the packages and the smiles they've brought. I cannot tell how much your kindness and support means to this unit. Every soldier here appreciates what you and everyone else back home are doing to support us during this difficult time. The care packages not only provided our soldiers with some comforts they cannot get over here, but also served as a reminder of the tireless support back home. It is hard to leave our family and friends behind, but your support makes it easier for us to complete our mission.

We have a tough, but important mission here in Mosul. We are a Military Police Company of about 180 soldiers that are responsible for the rebuilding, training, and equipping the Iraqi Police in Mosul. There are over 5000 police officers in and around the city, spread over 40 police stations. This is a lot of work for 180 people! However, we have some of the best soldiers in the Army that work hard everyday and do an outstanding job.

The 293d Military Police Company is one of the most deployed MP units in the Army today. This deployment is their third since September 11, 2001. The unit has also deployed to the Pentagon in Washington, D.C. and to Bagram, Afghanistan. Our current deployment to Iraq is expected last until March of 2005.

Thank you again for keeping our soldiers in your thoughts. We couldn't complete our mission if it wasn't for the support of people like you.

Warriors!

Sincerely,

Jason R. Jajack
Captain, U.S. Army
Commander

230

Certificates and Awards

DEPARTMENT OF THE ARMY
Bravo Company, 8th Engineer Battalion
5th BCT, 1st Cavalry Division
Camp Ferrin-Huggins, Iraq

LETTER FOR SOLDIERS ANGEL'S   3 February 2005

SUBJECT: Letter of appreciation for your support of **Operation Iraqi Freedom II March 04-
March 05.**

Soldiers of B Company 8th Engineer Battalion (combat engineers) would like to thank
you for your support in sending care packages or mail for our soldiers. Our unit is from Ft
Hood, TX. We are currently located in Baghdad, Iraq in the AL-RASHEED district. Our
website is www.8engineers.org press on "**wardogs**" icon it has not been updated but it will
give an idea of who we are and do.

Some of the current duties our soldiers perform include cordon and search operations,
traffic checkpoints, terrain analysis (map making), base camp security, route clearance and
search for Improvised Explosive Devices (IED's), location of enemy forces and
apprehension of insurgents, Iraqi infrastructure security to included supervision of the sewer
system operations, trash collection and electricity.

You are one of the many that has supported us for that we THANK YOU it makes a lot
of difference in our morale. The soldiers go on the streets all the time come back shower and
rest to be ready for next mission most of the time. We created this letter as a appreciation
from the soldiers of B Company 8 ENG BN Thanking you for your support. **We will not be
receiving any mail after 1 Feb 2005 due to redeployment.** Thank you for your support and
your prayers.

SALOMON GUERRA JR.
SFC, US
Operations Sergeant

TASK FORCE LIBERTY

April 14, 2005

Soldiers Angel
C/O Patti Bader
1792 E. Washington Blvd.
Pasadena, CA 91104

Dear Patti:

On behalf of the soldiers here at Task Force Liberty in Tikrit, Iraq, I would like to extend my warmest thank you for your letter and phone cards. It is nice to have a bit of "home" here in Iraq. I have sent the cards out to be distributed to soldiers who need them to be able to call their loved ones back home. I am hoping that each one will write to you to show their appreciation. It warms my heart to know that there are so many people back in the good old U.S.A. who care about the soldiers here in Iraq. People like you make it easier to be here. I am in the Division Headquarters here in Tikrit, Iraq. About 98% of the 42 ID is in Iraq. I will say a special prayer, everyday, for you. You will always have a special place in our hearts. We hope to finish our mission here and get back home as soon as we can. Until then, keep us in your hearts and your prayers.

Sincerely,

LTC Frantz Michel
G7, Task Force Liberty

Certificates and Awards

DEPARTMENT OF DEFENSE
COMBINED JOINT SPECIAL OPERATIONS TASK FORCE-
ARABIAN PENINSULA
BOX 5
APO AE 09391

Dear Ana-Marie and Patti Bader,

My name is Staff Sergeant Sar. I worked with an Army's chaplain. Together, the two of us, we are the Religious Support Team (RST). Our goals and objectives are to provide religious support, guard and guarantee freedom of religious to all soldiers, and advice the commander concerning the moral and morale of soldiers in the unit. Here in Iraq, we have a Chapel for Sunday Worship Service and Bible Study every Sunday and Saturday. In additional to the Chapel, we have Chaplain Center. The Chaplain Center is open 24/7 for soldiers to find a bit of comfort after a long day of work or returning from patrol, convoy and combat, a place to call home and a place to relax. We provide coffee, cookies, noodle, and reading literature to soldiers of all ranks and ages, 24/7.

The purpose of this letter is to inform you that I have received your precious gifts. Truly from the bottom of my heart and the same from all the soldiers here, I want to thank you, send you my blessing and I am eternal grateful. Please continue to support our troops fighting for freedom and liberating the oppressed. It is a sacrifice we are willing to make to protect our way of life and the freedom cherish every day. God bless you always.

EL K. SAR
SSG, USA
CJSOTF-AP RST NCOIC

233

May No Soldier Go Unloved

MAJOR GENERAL PETER W. CHIARELLI
COMMANDING GENERAL, 1ST CAVALRY DIVISION

requests the pleasure of your company

at a

Retreat Ceremony

in honor of the

First Cavalry Division Association Reunion

on Friday, the twenty-fourth of June

at four-thirty in the evening

1ˢᵗ Cavalry Division Parade Field
Fort Hood, Texas

R.S.V.P. by 17 June 2005   *Military: Duty Uniform*
(254) 287-9730/DSN 737-9730   *Civilian: Casual*
1cdrsvp@hood.army.mil

Certificates and Awards

OFFICE OF THE COMMANDING GENERAL
ATTN: PROTOCOL
1ST CAVALRY DIVISION
BUILDING 28000 72ND ST
FORT HOOD, TEXAS 76544
OFFICIAL BUSINESS

JUN 15 05   Ξ 0 3 7 Ξ

SOLDIERS ANGELS
1792 EAST WASHINGTON BLVD
PASADENA, CA 91104

3110442781 54

At this ceremony MG Chiarelli would like to personally recognize your organization for its support of the First Cavalry Division during its deployment to Operation Iraqi Freedom.

Please contact CPT Lucas Cioffi at 254/681-9651 with the name of the individual who may accept an award on behalf of your organization.

Thank You,
1st Cavalry Division Protocol

May No Soldier Go Unloved

THE WHITE HOUSE

WASHINGTON

August 2, 2005

Mr. Jeff Bader
Soldiers' Angels
Pasadena, California

Dear Jeff:

Thank you for your letter and the American flag. I appreciate your kind gesture and thoughtfulness.

Thanks as well for the good work you do to encourage and support our troops. Your compassion and service reflect the great character of our Nation.

Laura and I send our best wishes. May God bless you, and may God continue to bless America.

Sincerely,

George W. Bush

Certificates and Awards

Guardian Angels For Soldier's Pet
1331 Airport Rd., PMB# 169 – Hot Springs, AR 71913-8024
(501) 760-1801 or (501) 760-3875
Email: info@guardianangelsforsoldierspet.org
Website: www.guardianangelsforsoldierspet.org
All Volunteer 501(c) (3) Nonprofit – EIN: 20-2229425

President: Jim Olmedo   **Secretary:** Linda Johnson
Vice-President: Jorge Garcia, Jr   **Treasurer:** Linda Spurlin-Dominik
Directors: Carole Olmedo and Kay Ellis

October 12, 2005

Patti Patton-Bader
Soldiers' Angels
1792 E. Washington Blvd
Pasadena, CA 91104

Dear Patti,

Thank you for your gracious donation to our organization. and a small "Thank You" and recognition for your support to help us fulfill our mission.

Have great news! Not sure if you remember Sarah Vaughn (txmediclady), a Soldiers' Angel who signed up to be a medic from Texas in March 05 and is currently deployed in Kuwait. Sarah emailed our organization Monday about needing to find a temporary home for her 2 cats (Cleo and Tabby). A friend had been caring for them, but is unable to continue. We have arranged for a foster home for them here in Hot Springs and final arrangements are being made now to bring them to Hot Springs.

I am so happy we were able to help one of our own and a hero and friend to many in SA.

Since we were not called on to help pets affected by Katrina, the donation you made will be used towards providing food and other items to ensure that Sarah's beloved pets are cared for in a caring and loving home til she returns.

In closing I have also included a membership to "Guardian Angels For Soldier's Pet".

Again many thanks for all you do for our deployed heroes, SA, and our organization.

Linda D.
Linda Dominik
co-Founder/Treasurer
Guardian Angels For Soldier's Pet

Enclosures: Receipt # 865215 for $100 Donation
              GASP Membership Card
              Certificate of Appreciation

May No Soldier Go Unloved

UNDER SECRETARY OF DEFENSE
4000 DEFENSE PENTAGON
WASHINGTON, D.C. 20301-4000

PERSONNEL AND
READINESS

DEC 1 2 2005

Mr. Don MacKay
General Manager
Soldiers' Angels
1792 East Washington Blvd.
Pasadena, CA 91104

Dear Mr. MacKay:

Since February 1, 2005, the Department's Military Severely Injured Center has supported Service members who have been severely injured in the war on terror. We have been working hard to support their families. We realize the important role nonprofit organizations play in caring for the severely injured. The myriad services that your volunteers provide contribute significantly to the recovery process of the severely injured. Often, financial assistance, transportation, housing, family and other community services would not have been possible without your support.

Our severely injured personnel and their families know that America cares about their sacrifices. Thank you for your continued support of our nation's heroes.

Sincerely,

David S. C. Chu

238

Certificates and Awards

DEPARTMENT OF VETERANS AFFAIRS
Veterans Health Administration
Washington DC 20420

JAN 2 5 2006

In Reply Refer To: 10C2

Ms. Patti Bader
Founder, Soldiers Angels
1792 East Washington Blvd.
Pasadena, CA 91104

Dear Ms. Bader:

I sincerely thank you for your generous donation of the personal laptop computers to returning Iraqi combat soldiers. This donation will allow our patients and their families to be better informed about their disability and to stay connected to their families and friends. It was a pleasure to meet members of your organization and to personally thank them last month.

I was pleased to learn of your organization's recent visit to the VA Medical Center in Richmond to tour our Polytrauma Center, and that the representatives were able to present donated laptops to the patients recovering at the facility. I understand that the computers were very well received by our patients and their families, and I hope your members found the visit to be worthwhile.

Your generosity in raising the funds and for securing support of the Military Order of Purple Heart and Dell Corporation are truly appreciated. Thank you for your efforts in support of America's greatest heroes—our Nation's veterans.

Sincerely yours,

Jonathan B. Perlin, MD, PhD, MSHA, FACP
Under Secretary for Health

May No Soldier Go Unloved

DEPARTMENT OF THE ARMY
Medical Task Force 10
Baghdad, Iraq
APO, AE 09348

February 3, 2006

REPLY TO
ATTENTION OF

Commander

Patti Bader (Soldiers' Angels)
1792 E. Washington Blvd.
Pasadena, CA 91104

Dear Patti:

I would like to take this opportunity to express my sincere appreciation and gratitude for the outstanding contribution that you made to the 10th Combat Support Hospital during Operation Iraqi Freedom 05-07.

Your selfless dedication will make a difference in our mission; your support will have a direct and significant impact on our ability to provide world-class healthcare to our patients. The packages containing socks are immensely important to the well-being of our patients and bring a welcome feel of comfort and caring to Soldiers sick or injured in a far-away place. Your loyal support and assistance as an American contribute immeasurably to the success of the 10th Combat Support Hospital.

Again, I want to thank you personally for your patriotic support. It would be a great pleasure to have you as a member of any organization that I may be associated with in the future. Thank you again on behalf of all the Soldiers in the greatest Army in the world.

Sincerely,

Dennis D. Doyle
Colonel, US Army
Commanding

240

Certificates and Awards

THE SECRETARY OF DEFENSE
WASHINGTON

FEB 8 2006

Ms. Patti Patton-Bader
Soldiers' Angels
1792 East Washington Boulevard
Pasadena, CA 91104

Dear Ms. Patton-Bader,

I want to express my appreciation for the invaluable support you provide to our men and women in uniform. As a member of the "America Supports You" team, your organization helps strengthen the bonds between our military and the Americans they serve.

Thank you for letting service members and their families know how much their fellow Americans value their courage, commitment and sacrifice.

Sincerely,

May No Soldier Go Unloved

February 09, 2006

Patti Bader
Soldier's Angels
1792 East Washington Blvd,
Pasadena, CA 91104

Dear Mrs. Bader,

Thank you for your tremendous support in resourcing the hotel accommodation of several of our severely wounded soldiers who attended the National Football League's Super Bowl XL. This lifetime dream simply would not have been possible had you not recognized the need and volunteered on the spot to cover the hotel portion of the trip.

I deeply appreciate the commitment of the Soldier's Angels to our military. Thank you and the Soldier's Angels – from the men and women of the United States Armed Forces and the entire Department of Defense. Please find enclosed a coin from the Deputy Secretary of Defense and the thanks from all those assigned to the Office of the Deputy Secretary of Defense.

Sincerely,

Frank G. Helmick
BG, USA
Senior Military Assistant to the
Deputy Secretary of Defense

Many Thanks!
Mary

DEPARTMENT OF THE ARMY
TASK FORCE SOUTH, MEDICAL TASK FORCE 10
ALI AIR BASE, IRAQ
APO AE 09331

REPLY TO
ATTENTION OF

21 February, 2006

Commander, Task Force South

Ms. Patti Bader
c/o Soldiers' Angels
1792 East Washington Boulevard
Pasadena, CA 91104

Dear Ms. Bader,

I am writing to thank you for the socks and gifts that you and Soldiers' Angels sent to my Soldiers. Your kind gifts were very much appreciated and enjoyed by all, and they have helped both ourselves and the patients to whom we provide care here in Southern Iraq. Thank you once again for taking the time to think of us and for providing such outstanding support for my Soldiers as we serve on freedom's frontier.

Sincerely,

Ralph W. Deatherage
Major, US Army
Commanding

May No Soldier Go Unloved

Commanding General
101st Airborne Division (Air Assault)

February 21, 2006

Dear Soldiers Angels,

On behalf of the Soldiers and families of the 101st Airborne Division (Air Assault), I would like to personally thank you for your tremendous generosity. The laptop computers you donated for our Soldiers and their families to use have made a tremendous impact. It is the selfless actions of people like you that make serving our great nation such an honor.

Sincerely,

Thomas R. Turner
Major General, USA
Commanding

Soldiers Angels
1792 East Washington Blvd.
Pasadena, CA 91104

Certificates and Awards

DEPARTMENT OF THE AIR FORCE
332 EXPEDITIONARY LOGISTICS READINESS SQUADRON, DETACHMENT 2
Q-WEST, IRAQ, APO AE 09334

27 February 2006

332 ELRS, DET 2
AEF 9/10 JACOT
Q-West Base Complex
APO AE 09334

Soldier's Angels
C/O Patti Bader
1792 E. Washington Blvd.
Pasadena, CA 91104

Dear Ms Bader and Soldier's Angels

Thank you so much for your support of the troops and your generous gift. You have sacrificed your time to ensure we are not forgotten and I cannot think of a more selfless act. Please extend a sincere THANK YOU to all of those who made this possible on behalf of the Airmen I serve with, and all other military members deployed world wide. What you do from the heart, means so much to all of us. It may seem like a small thing to some, but believe me, it is something that we will NEVER forget. I hope that you will always be able to look back and feel good about all that you have done to make us feel that much closer to home.

Let me tell you a little bit about us…we are an Air Force Detachment with 28 personnel responsible for Aerial Port Operations at Qayyarah West, Iraq, also know as "Q-West." The Team consists of a Logistics Readiness Officer, Command and Control, Radio Communications, Aerial Porters, Aircraft Maintainers, Vehicle Maintainers, and Aerospace Ground Equipment Maintainers. We arrived here on 15 Jan 06 and will be here for 120 days as part of Aerospace Expeditionary Force 9/10. The majority of the team are assigned to Charleston AFB, SC; however, we have folks from Kirtland AFB, NM, Dobbins AFB, GA, Hill AFB, UT, McChord AFB, WA, Lackland AFB, TX, Eglin AFB, FL, and as far away as RAF Mildenhall in the United Kingdom, and Yokota AB and Kadena AB in Japan.

We work on the Airfield and primarily handle C-130 Hercules and C-17 Globemaster aircraft. Our work site is fairly basic; however, we try to make improvements everyday. We live in Containerized Housing Units that we call CHU's. We have "cadillac" shower and toilet units, which basically means we have running water in the showers and toilets that flush. At our work site and throughout the rest of the base, we have porta potties. The dining facility is pretty good; there is a good selection of entrees and desserts, and we even have baskin robins ice cream. We also have Meals Ready To Eat (or MREs) when we can't make it to the dining facility.

For leisure activities, we have a Recreation Center located in a large tent with a full screen movie theater, TVs, games, computers, telephones, and a small Library. We also have a Fitness Center in a tent with a basketball court, cardiovascular, and weight rooms. These areas stay very busy as they are the only recreational facilities available on the base. There is also a Turkish Mall that sells some items from Turkey.

Right now, it is the rainy season in Iraq and mud is everywhere. We have experienced thunder, lightning, and even hail. We are looking forward to the dry season to start so we can experience the sandstorms too. ☺ Again, thank you so much for your generosity and supporting the troops! All the best from the Can Do Crew at the "Q."

Sincerely,

KELLIE L. DAVILA-MARTINEZ, Lt Col, USAF
Commander

May No Soldier Go Unloved

DEPARTMENT OF THE ARMY
ALPHA COMPANY, BRIGADE SPECIAL TROOPS BATTALION
1ST HEAVY BRIGADE COMBAT TEAM, 2D INFANTRY DIVISION
UNIT #15108
APO AP 96224-5108

EAID-FB-BTB-ACO

1 March 6, 2006

Dear Friends of the Assassins,

Thank you for your support this past Christmas holiday. I apologize for this letter being late, we never seem to have the time to stop and focus on the things that matter; like thanking the folks at home who support us on a daily basis. The tardiness of these thanks is entirely my fault and should have been done much longer ago.

Your cards, letters and care packages were well received by my Soldiers and exemplified the untiring and patriotic spirit of the American people. There is no doubt that America supports its men and women serving in uniform. It makes me proud to know that there are outstanding folks and organizations at home that find the time, are willing to make the sacrifice, and who genuinely care about their troops abroad.

These are definitely trying times for our Armed Forces as we find ourselves spread across the globe laying the foundations of freedom and protecting the American way of life. For many of my Soldiers, this was their first Christmas away from home and for others it was their first holiday season separated from their families. Your generous gifts and warm wishes brought the holiday spirit to my Company and made a difference in their lives.

Unfortunately, I lack the eloquence and poetry to actually describe the joy that your letters and gifts brought to my Soldiers. But rest assured that there were many smiles and tender thoughts as they read each letter and card. We also made sure that each Soldier received a care package and Christmas card. Any excess gifts or cards were forwarded to troops serving in Afghanistan and Iraq, so your love and caring spread much farther than South Korea.

I have enclosed a unit coin to express my thanks and make you honorary members of the Assassin team. Without your support at home, our jobs would be much harder and good morale much harder to achieve.

Sincerely,

YUKIO A. KUNIYUKI III
CPT, MI
Commanding

Certificates and Awards

**Commanding General
United States Army Special Forces Command (Airborne)
Fort Bragg, North Carolina 28310**

March 7, 2006

Dear Ms. Bader:

    I am writing to you, both personally and on behalf of the Special Forces Regiment, to recognize and thank you and the Soldier's Angels Foundation for your outstanding assistance provided to our wounded Soldiers and their families. Please accept my sincere thanks and deepest, heartfelt gratitude for your tremendous support of these brave men and women.

    The aid and comfort your foundation has provided, in arranging transportation for loved ones to and from Walter Reed Army Hospital, and the monetary donations given to help them defray the extra costs incurred during their stays in the DC area, have had a tremendous impact on their morale and well being. The voice-activated laptop computers the foundation gave to Soldiers with devastating injuries, that prevented them from using conventional keyboards, were especially useful and very much appreciated.

    In closing, thank you again for all you and the volunteers of the Soldier's Angels Foundation have done and continue to do for our Soldiers and their families.

                Sincerely,

                John F. Mulholland
                Brigadier General, US Army
                Commanding

Ms. Patti Bader
Founder
Soldier's Angels Foundation
1792 East Washington Blvd
Pasadena, California 91104

247

May No Soldier Go Unloved

DEPARTMENT OF THE AIR FORCE
332 EXPEDITIONARY LOGISTICS READINESS SQUADRON, DETACHMENT 2
Q-WEST, IRAQ, APO AE 09334

31 March 2006

332 ELRS, DET 2
AEF 9/10 JACOT
Q-West Base Complex
APO AE 09334

Soldier's Angels
1792 E. Washington Blvd
Pasadena, CA 91104

Dear Soldiers Angels

I wanted to let you know how much I appreciate what your organization has done to support our unit in Qayyarah West, Iraq. Your care packages and lettersw were a wonderful surprise and I can't say thank you enough for the kindness your organization has shown to all of us! I know that the members of your organization have sacrificed their personal time to make us all feel a little closer to home and we all appreciate it! I would also like to thank you for the wonderful Soldier's Angels coin that you recently sent to us. We received it today.

I thought you might like to know a little bit about me. I am the 377th Logistics Readiness Squadron Commander at Kirtland AFB, New Mexico. I have over 250 people that work in Transportation (Vehicle Operations, Vehicle Maintenance, Traffic Management), Supply, Fuels, Logistics Plans, and Aerial Port Operations. I've been in the military as a Transportation and Logistics Officer for almost 20 years. It's hard to believe that 28 May 06 is my 20th anniversary. I love being a Commander – I have had the opportunity twice – first, at Incirlik AB, Turkey in 2001 and now at Kirtland AFB, New Mexico. As you may know, our deployment in Iraq ends in mid May and I will return to Albuquerque for about three weeks. I will be heading to Norfolk, Virginia to attend school for ten weeks and then I'll be off to Izmir, Turkey for my new assignment. I will be there for one year before I move on to an assignment in Germany, at least that's the current plan.

I have two younger brothers and one younger sister who all live in/around Flint, Michigan along with my mom and dad. I have a niece and a nephew and another niece due to arrive in June. I love to travel, sightsee, go to Flea Markets, Craft Fairs, make beaded jewelry, and rollerblade. I love all different kinds of music, but my favorites are Soul Classics, R&B, and Country. I also love to go to concerts and the theater for musicals.

Anyway, our time here is more than half over. It's amazing how fast the time has gone. We stay busy, whether we are dowloading or uploading passengers and cargo on aircraft, building additional office space, or improving security on the airfield. The rains have stopped and we are in the dry season now. We've already had a couple of sandstorms. I'm not 100% sure, but I think I might like the rain better. Again, many thanks for your kindness and taking the time out of your busy schedule to make us all feel at home. ☺

KELLIE L. DAVILA-MARTINEZ, Lt Col, USAF
Commander, 332 ELRS, Det 2

Certificates and Awards

DEPARTMENT OF THE ARMY
440TH SIGNAL BATTALION
APO AE, 09342

July 26, 2006

Commander, 440th Signal Battalion

Patti Patton-Bader
Soldiers' Angels Foundation
1792 E. Washington Boulevard
Pasadena, California 91104

Debby Frerichs
Director Central Region Soldiers' Angels
3208 SW Alice Lane
Lees Summit, Missouri 64082-4067

Dear Ms. Patton-Bader and Ms. Frerichs:

I want to offer my profound thanks for the wonderful support the Soldiers' Angels organization has provided to Task Force Runner this past year. Your volunteers have continually brightened the lives of my deployed Soldiers by sending packages, letters and gifts while they deal with the arduous conditions of combat in the desert.

My soldiers have benefited from the unsolicited support you have given them. The cool scarves have made our duties more comfortable in the heat of the Middle East. The replacement boots, multi-tools, flashlights and many other comfort items sent to the troops from Soldiers' Angels have made a tremendous impact on our ability to work safely and efficiently on the battlefield. Many of my remote sites lack a post exchange, so the gifts of toiletry and entertainment items have been a welcome respite.

Most of all, the communication between your sponsors and the Soldiers, and the willingness of the sponsors to meet the Soldier's needs has been the hallmark of Soldiers' Angels. Your Soldiers' Angles have ensured my Soldiers don't just get boxes of unwanted items a drug store can't sell. I'm continually impressed that your sponsors have gone out of their way to provide quality, name brand items for my troops, even when it was more expensive or time consuming to do so.

Soldiers' Angels has proven to be a wonderful organization, filled with people who are deeply concerned about Soldiers deployed all over the world. I say thank you again to all of your volunteers for the tremendous support and outpouring of love they

-2-

have given my Soldiers. I hope and pray that Soldiers' Angels will continue to provide the same level of support to the Soldiers who will follow us.

Sincerely,

Derek T. Orndorff
Lieutenant Colonel
Battalion Commander

Certificates and Awards

DEPARTMENT OF THE AIR FORCE
332 Air Force Theater Hospital
Balad Air Base, Iraq

22 Aug 06

Soldiers' Angels
1792 E. Washington Blvd
Pasadena, CA 91104

Dear Soldiers' Angels,

On behalf of 332d Expeditionary Aerospace Medicine Squadron (EAMDS), I would like to personally thank you for the generous donations of Crystal Light drink mix and coffee and support that your organization provided for our injured war heroes who are awaiting airlift transportation to a safer area. Your continued commitment in providing for our troops is sincerely appreciated by the troops themselves, their families back home, and the Contingency Aeromedical Staging Facility (CASF) medical staff.

One of the many missions of the CASF is to provide the incoming heroes with a quiet resting area, warm shower, clean change of clothes, and the small but meaningful extras that remind the troops just how much we love and support them. Donations from supporters like you, and your family help to ensure our heroes are comfortable and well taken care of as they continue their homeward journey.

I would like to personally acknowledge your support for our troops and can not begin to tell you how much your support means to all of us. To know that we are remembered is a wonderful gift. Thank you again for your generous donations and continued support.

Mike L. Bunning, Col, USAF, BSC
332 EAMDS Commander
Balad/LSA Anaconda, Iraq
APO AE 09315-9997

251

May No Soldier Go Unloved

DEPARTMENT OF VETERANS AFFAIRS
Medical Center
7305 North Military Trail
West Palm Beach FL 33410-6400

November 13, 2006

In Reply Refer To:
548/135

Ms. Patti Bador
Soldier's Angels
1792 E. Washington Blvd.
Pasadena, CA 91104

Dear Ms. Bador:

On behalf of the Department of Veterans Affairs Medical Center, West Palm Beach, Florida, I would like to take this opportunity to thank you and the members of your organization for the recent donation of 13 pairs of sun and reading glasses for visitors to the Fisher House.

Once again, I would like to thank you for supporting our veterans. If you have any questions or need any additional information, please contact Voluntary Service at (561) 422-7373.

Sincerely yours,

Mary C. Phillips

Mary C. Phillips, Chief
Voluntary/Recreation Therapy Service

Certificates and Awards

DEPARTMENT OF THE ARMY
1ST BATTALION, 505TH PARACHUTE INFANTRY REGIMENT, 82D AIRBORNE DIVISION
FOB SUMMERALL, BAYJI, IRAQ
APO AE 09393

Office of the Battalion Commander   17 November 2006
1st Battalion, 505th Parachute Infantry Regiment
82nd Airborne Division
FOB Summerall, APO AE 09393

Soldier's Angels
ATTN: Ms. Patti Bader
1792 E. Washington Blvd.
Pasadena, CA 91104

Dear Ms. Bader,

I wanted to send you a note thanking you for the AT&T phone cards you sent me. As you may or may not know, I am the Commander of Task Force 1-505 from 3rd Brigade of the 82nd Airborne Division. I have approximately 1,000 Paratroopers that work for me in Bayji, Iraq at Forward Operating Base (FOB) Summerall. I passed the cards out to lucky Paratroopers from the Task Force.

A soldier's ability to talk to friends and family back in the United States is cherished. Your kind donation will allow Troopers to call from our AT&T phone center here on the FOB to their loved ones. I thank you from the bottom of my heart and so do my Troopers. It is nice to know that people back home care about us.

We are trying to do our part to fight the war on terrorism. I just ask that you keep my men in your thoughts and prayers as they continue to do the job our Nation has asked them to do. They won't ask for anything in return, just the knowledge that people care.

Thank you once again for generous donation to the Troopers of Task Force 1-505.

Scott A. Harris
Lieutenant Colonel, Infantry
Commanding

May No Soldier Go Unloved

DEPARTMENT OF THE ARMY
Alpha Company, 303rd Military Intelligence Battalion
APO, AE 09342

AFVQ-OP-A

28 November 2006

To all who have so generously supported Alpha Company,

Thank You!! Your support has been tremendous and is so graciously appreciated by all the Soldiers in our unit. We can't tell you how much it means to us that you care and took the time to send the care packages and letters to our Soldiers. They are working hard, 24/7 and morale is high this holiday season.

The items in each package were disseminated accordingly to the Soldiers needing them. The toiletry items are always hot as the local exchange here is frequently out of stock on those items. The food, games, and books – again, thank you. It is all distributed and appreciated. Although the Soldiers are working long hours here, it's nice to play a game of cards, roll some dice, or to read a good book when the opportunity is afforded.

For those who send toys, they are also put to good use. The military police and Marine Corps have teamed up this year to run the Toys for Tots campaign. The toys are donated to these units and distributed to local orphanages, schools, and troops on patrol.

Many of you also donated holiday decorations. Truthfully, this seems to have lifted the Soldiers' spirits here most. Despite the stress of the job day in and day out, you can't help but be happy to walk into your work area that is decked out in festive décor. Sunday we even had a tree-trimming ceremony using all the wonderful decorations sent by our supporters and well-wishers back home. While we wish we could be with our own families during this season, it is nice to get together with our brothers and sisters in arms for such special occasions. Again, thank you.

We wish each and every one of you the best this holiday season and into the New Year. Your continued support in the form of cards, letters, and small packages keeps our troops focused, knowing that their mission here is an important one and still supported by our fellow Americans back home. You are why we serve proudly and continue to drive forward in order to accomplish our mission. We look forward to each day knowing we are doing our best and look forward to when we can once again return home to spend quality time with our loved ones and fellow Patriots.

Sincerely,

Kristen Anderson
SFC, USA
First Sergeant

Brian Cunningham
CPT, MI
Commander

DEPARTMENT OF THE ARMY
2ND BATTALION, 227TH AVIATION REGIMENT
1ST AIR CAVALRY BRIGADE, 1ST CAVALRY DIVISION
CAMP TAJI, IRAQ APO AE 09378

REPLY TO
ATTENTION OF

December 13, 2006

Office of the Battalion Chaplain

Soldiers' Angels
C/O Melissa Brink
15311 State HWY 205
Terrell, TX 75160

Dear Melissa:

Thank you for the care packages you sent. We began receiving them late November, 2006. The soldiers really appreciate the sacrifice you make to send them care package. The travel mugs are a big hit!

Our unit is very special; we do missions that no one else is capable of performing. One mission we perform is moving key leaders and VIPs throughout the Baghdad area. Most soldiers in Baghdad will ride on one of our helicopters as they prepare to go on R-n-R or return home at the end of their tour. We also transport the soldiers that are coming in to the greater Baghdad area so others can return home. We also save many lives with our medical evacuation helicopters. Wounded US soldiers, coalition forces, civilians, and enemy forces are picked up and taken to the hospital. Our helicopters also transport mail in and around Baghdad so your care packages can make it to the soldiers and their letters can make it home.

As you can see we do a lot of different missions. To make the mission happen we rely on soldiers with different types of skills. Some soldiers act like operators, recording and relaying all relevant radio messages. We have some soldiers that repair helicopters, while others repair ground vehicles necessary to keep the helicopters flying. There are soldiers that refuel the helicopters and others that man the guns to protect them as they fly. We have officers and warrant officers that fly the helicopters and manage various aspects of the mission. Many more soldiers and officers perform other tasks necessary to the mission but to list them all would take too long.

All of the soldiers appreciate heroes and heroines like you, people who take time out of their busy lives to express care and concern for those who are doing their job here in Iraq and elsewhere.

The Commander and Sergeant Major express their appreciation for your efforts as well.

Thank You for Your Support,

Andrew K. Arrington
Chaplain (Captain) US Army
Battalion Chaplain

May No Soldier Go Unloved

DEPARTMENT OF THE AIR FORCE
Pacific Air Force

15 December 2006

Soldiers' Angels
Attn: Mrs. Patti Bader
1792 E. Washington Blvd.
Pasadena, CA 91104

Chaplain, Captain Herbert C. Shao
451 AEG Chaplain
APO, AE 09355

Dear Mrs. Bader,

On behalf of the 451 Air Expeditionary Group, I would like to thank you for your donation of hot chocolate mix. Your generosity and kindness will help increase the morale of the airmen serving here in Afghanistan during the holidays. Every little bit makes a tremendous difference!

If I can be so bold as to make one request, please keep our coalition forces as well as the people of Afghanistan in your prayers—that peace will prevail with the least amount of lives sacrificed. Thank you once again. May our God continue to bless you richly.

Respectfully,

HERBERT C. SHAO
Chaplain, Captain, USAF

Certificates and Awards

ARMY FISHER HOUSES

December 29, 2006

Patti Bader
1792 E Washington Blvd
Pasadena, CA 91104

Dear Patti Bader,

On behalf of the Walter Reed Army Medical Center (WRAMC) Fisher House staff and residents, I would like to thank you for your most generous donation. Your generosity will assist us in our continuous effort to provide our combat soldiers and their families with the very best care. Our program includes lodging at no cost; unlimited supplies of food; beverages; clothing; diapers and other baby and children necessities; toiletries; calling cards, and any other items they may need. Furthermore, we provide our service member with assistive technology, resource organization information, and support group therapy.

Our goal is to make the service member and their families comfortable and secure in a nurturing environment that will assist them in their transition back to civilian life.

All of us at the WRAMC Fisher Houses wish you all the best and thank you for your support!

Sincerely,

Kathryn A. Deyermond
Manager, WRAMC
Fisher Houses

WALTER REED FISHER HOUSE • 6900 GEORGIA AVENUE, N.W. • WASHINGTON DC 20307
PHONE: 202 545-3218 • FAX: 202 545-3202

Charitable contributions provide the majority of funding for the Army Fisher Houses.
Please visit us at www.armyfisherhouses.org.

257

May No Soldier Go Unloved

Fisher House
Incorporated
Assisting military families in medical crisis

January 2, 2007

Ms. Patti Bader
Soldiers' Angels
1792 E. Washington Blvd.
Pasadena, CA 91104

Dear Ms. Bader and members of the Soldiers' Angels:

On behalf of our Board of Directors, we would like to thank you for providing the Lackland Fisher House residents with three boxes of "mini" stuffed bears. Words can not adequately express our appreciation of the giving of your precious time and gifts.

There is no greater responsibility than caring for others and over the past fourteen years, the Lackland Fisher Houses have been able to do this only through the ongoing generosity of donors like you. Fisher House, Inc. and our residents appreciate your kind support in this regard.

Your donation helps us "be there" for military families by alleviating some of the financial and emotional hardship during their medical crisis. Thank you for your continued support.

Sincerely,

Raymond T. Holmes
Executive Director

NOTE: IRS rules require us to advise you that no goods or services were provided in consideration of this gift and, for tax purposes, this letter serves as your receipt. Fisher House is a 501(c) (3) charitable organization as defined by the IRS code and gifts are normally tax deductible. In calculating the tax liability, the valuation of non-cash items is the responsibility of the donor.

7323 Highway 90 West, Suite 107 San Antonio, Texas 78227-3662
(210) 673-7500 • (210) 673-7579 fax
fisherhouseinc@sbcglobal.net
www.fisherhouseinc.org

Certificates and Awards

DEPARTMENT OF THE AIR FORCE
732D EXPEDITIONARY SECURITY FORCES SQUADRON
BALAD AIR BASE IRAQ

Soldiers' Angel,

I want to personally thank you for the time and effort you gave in what I believe to be a dramatic display of support from the home front.

The 732d Expeditionary Security Forces Squadron serves a very unique mission in Iraq. There are Officers, Enlisted and K9 Airman scattered all over Iraq in more than 30 locations. Many of these Airmen do not have the opportunity to visit our simplified version of Walmart, the Base Exchange, to pick up the basic necessities, have a phone to call home or a computer to email. Your generous support provided a heartfelt reminder that we are proudly serving our great nation in the fight against terrorism. My squadron is distributing these packages, letters and pictures to airmen who may get little or no mail. This provides them a brief moment to think of home and know there are people that care about the lives of our airmen in combat.

On behalf of the men and women of the 732d Expeditionary Security Forces Squadron, I would like to thank you again for your heartfelt letters, pictures and packages.

BRETT A. MEYER, Lt Col, USAF
Commander

"Tip of the Spear"

May No Soldier Go Unloved

FAMILY READINESS GROUP
14th QUARTERMASTER COMPANY
900 ARMORY DRIVE
GREENSBURG, PA 15601

January 15, 2007

Soldiers Angels
Patti Patton Bader
1792 East Washington Blvd.
Pasadena, CA 91104

Dear Patti & all Soldiers' Angels:

We want to thank you for your generous and continuous support to our soldiers and their families throughout their mobilization and deployment in Iraq.

They are so proud to know they and their families were supported by their fellow citizens in so many ways. They always felt your love and concern...you truly are Soldiers' Angels!

Please accept the enclosed cookbook with sincere appreciation of all your efforts in behalf of soldiers and their families everywhere. Again, thank you and may God bless America!

Dorothy Benyacko Carbisiero, Leader
14th Quartermaster Company
Family Readiness Group

Certificates and Awards

DEPARTMENT OF THE ARMY
2ND BATTALION, 227TH AVIATION REGIMENT
1ST AIR CAVALRY BRIGADE, 1ST CAVALRY DIVISION
CAMP TAJI, IRAQ APO AE 09378

REPLY TO
ATTENTION OF

15 January 2007

Office of the Battalion Chaplain

Soldiers' Angels
17171 148th Avenue
Spring Lake, MI 49456-9514

Dear Patti Patton-Bader

Thank you for your work to establish and run Soldiers' Angels. We received many care packages from volunteers utilizing your organization. The Soldiers really appreciate the time and effort you and others put into sending them care packages.

Our unit is very special; we do missions that no one else is capable of performing. One mission we perform is moving key leaders and VIPs throughout the Baghdad area. Most Soldiers in Baghdad will ride on one of our helicopters as they prepare to go on R-n-R or return home at the end of their tour. We also transport the Soldiers that are coming in to the greater Baghdad area so others can return home. We also save many lives with our medical evacuation helicopters. Wounded US Soldiers, coalition forces, civilians, and enemy forces are picked up and taken to the hospital. Our helicopters also transport mail in and around Baghdad so your care packages can make it to the Soldiers and their letters can make it home.

As you can see we do a lot of different missions. To make the mission happen we rely on Soldiers with different types of skills. Some Soldiers act like operators, recording and relaying all relevant radio messages. We have some Soldiers that repair helicopters, while others repair ground vehicles necessary to keep the helicopters flying. There are Soldiers that refuel the helicopters and others that man the guns to protect them as they fly. We have officers and warrant officers that fly the helicopters and manage various aspects of the mission. Many more Soldiers and officers perform other tasks necessary to the mission but to list them all would take too long.

All of the Soldiers appreciate heroes and heroines like you, people who take time out of their busy lives to express care and concern for those who are doing their job here in Iraq and elsewhere.

The Commander and Sergeant Major express their appreciation for your efforts as well.

Thank You for Your Support,

Andrew K. Arrington
Chaplain (Captain) US Army
Battalion Chaplain

May No Soldier Go Unloved

DEPARTMENT OF THE ARMY
HEADQUARTERS AND HEADQUARTERS COMPANY
4ᵀᴴ BRIGADE SPECIAL TROOPS BATTALION (Airborne)
82ᴰᴰ AIRBORNE DIVISION
FORT BRAGG, NORTH CAROLINA 28310

REPLY TO
ATTENTION OF

AFVC-DF-HHC   01 March 2007

Dear Patti,

Thank you for your generous support of our Paratroopers! We could not accomplish our mission here without the support from our families and friends back home. Each letter or care package we receive makes us feel like the folks back home understand our dedication to this country and their development into a self-sustaining nation. We have been overwhelmed by the huge amount of support we are receiving not only from those back home, but from the people of Afghanistan- it truly helps us stay motivated!

Let us tell you a little about ourselves: we are the Headquarters and Headquarters Company (HHC) of the 508ᵗʰ Special Troops Battalion (STB) of the 4ᵗʰ Brigade Combat Team (BCT) of the 82d Airborne Division, based out of beautiful Fort Bragg, North Carolina. We have roughly 100 Paratroopers on a very small and remote Fire Base (FB) in a beautiful central Province in Afghanistan. We are comprised of mostly Military Policemen and women, a command and control element, an intelligence collection team, a civil-military coordination team, and various support personnel (cooks, mechanics, medics, etc).

We have the opportunity to assist in training the Afghan National Police (ANP) and we are extremely proud to work with such professionals who are truly dedicated to the security of their nation. It is our privilege to conduct joint security missions with them, including providing school supplies to children as the school year begins; providing much-needed food, clothing, and basic need items; and ensuring that the basic Law Enforcement functions are being conducted.

Our Company leadership is working closely with the ANP leadership and the Provincial government to determine where the areas of greatest need are and to ensure that the appropriate resources are committed to reach the desired effects. Resources are often sparse and allocated to the areas that are immediately affected. Unfortunately, this means that some resources, like school supplies for children (notebooks, pencils, erasers, etc.) or police equipment (tool belts, handcuffs, flashlights, basic life support items, etc.) are in very short supply.

In working so closely with the ANP we have come to truly appreciate their intriguing history and unique culture. We have worked hard to develop a "One Team, One Fight" attitude and this has been extremely successful! Attached are some pictures of our paratroopers in action and the heroes that we work with here in our Province. Please spread the word about all the good that we are accomplishing in cooperation with the ANP and please keep up the great support from the homefront!

LINDSAY R. C. MATTHEWS   KENNETH L. JACKSON
CPT, CM   1SG, USA
Commanding   First Sergeant

Thank you so much for the terrific care package! Supplies here are hard to come by as we are so far from an exchange! Thanks for your support! Lindsay

DEPARTMENT OF VETERANS AFFAIRS
North Texas Health Care System

In Reply Refer To: 549/135

March 16, 2007

Patti Bader
Soldiers Angels
1792 E. Washington Blvd.
Pasadena, CA 91104

Dear Ms. Bader:

On behalf of the VA North Texas Health Care System, Dallas VA Medical Center, I would like to thank you and your organization for your generous donation of pre-paid phone cards for our hospitalized veteran patients.

It is with support such as yours that we are able to make our veterans' stay in the hospital more pleasant and cheerful.

Again, thank you for your donation and your concern for our veterans.

Sincerely yours,

Betty Bolin Brown
Director

May No Soldier Go Unloved

Statue of appreciation from Ft. Bragg Fisher House

Certificates and Awards

Statue of appreciation from the Army National Guard

Certificate of Appreciation

is presented to

PATTI BADER

FOR YOUR OUTSTANDING PATRIOTISM AND KINDNESS IN
SUPPORT OF THE 10TH COMBAT SUPPORT HOSPITAL DURING
OPERATION IRAQI FREEDOM 05-07. YOUR GENEROUS
CONTRIBUTIONS TO THE STAFF AND PATIENTS OF THE 10TH
COMBAT SUPPORT HOSPITAL SIGNIFICANTLY ENHANCED THE
MORALE AND HEALTHCARE PROVIDED TO UNITED STATES
AND COALITION FORCES. YOUR DEDICATION AND SELFLESS
SERVICE REFLECT GREAT CREDIT UPON YOU, THE 10TH
COMBAT SUPPORT HOSPITAL AND THE UNITED STATES ARMY.

CY S. K. AKANA, CSM, USA
Command Sergeant Major

DENNIS D. DOYLE, COL, MS
Commanding

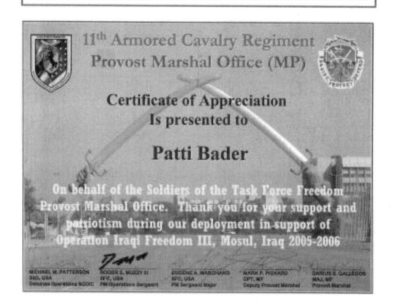

266

148th Support Battalion
48th Brigade Combat Team

CERTIFICATE OF APPRECIATION

AWARDED TO

SOLDIER'S ANGELS

FOR YOUR SUPPORT OF THE MEN AND WOMEN OF THE GEORGIA ARMY NATIONAL GUARD. WE WOULD LIKE TO TAKE THIS OPPORTUNITY TO SAY THANK YOU FOR YOUR CARING CONTRIBUTION OF GIFTS TO THE SOLDIERS. YOU WILL ALWAYS BE TRULY APPRECIATED BY THE 148TH SUPPORT BATTALION DURING OPERATION IRAQI FREEDOM III.

GIVEN THIS 19th DAY OF APRIL, 2006
AT CAMP ADDER, TALLIL AB, IRAQ

JESSE E. FAULKNER
CSM, USA
Command Sergeant Major

JEFFREY R. CLY
LTC, QM
Commanding

1st Cavalry Division

B COMPANY 8TH ENGINEER BATTALION
(COMBAT)
CERTIFICATE OF APPRECIATION
IS PRESENTED TO

Soldier's Angels

For your outstanding support during OPERATION IRAQI FREEDOM II. The soldiers in B Company, 8th Engineer Battalion, 1st Cavalry Division appreciate your support and love. Your generosity and dedication in sending mail and care packages has increased our unit's morale.

February 2004 thru February 2005

CARLOS E. AYUB
First Sergeant, USA

MATTHEW Y. McCULLEY
Commander, USA

Certificates and Awards

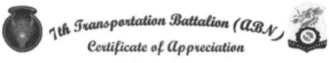

7th Transportation Battalion (ABN)
Certificate of Appreciation
Is presented to

The Soldier's Angels

For

Your sincere support to soldiers of the 7th Transportation Battalion during our deployment in support of Operation Iraqi Freedom IV. The patriotism and dedication you display by supporting our soldiers deployed in combat areas reflects your deep concern for our country and is greatly appreciated.
On Time, On Target!

CEPHUSE M. BAKER
CSM, USA
Command Sergeant Major

ALLEN W. KIEFER
LTC, QM
Commanding

United States Army
85th Division (Training Support)

COMMANDER'S AWARD

Presented to

Soldier's Angels

For outstanding service and immeasurable contributions to the 85th Division (Training Support). Your Operation Cookie Drop contributed to the success of the 85th Division in support of Operation Enduring Freedom and Noble Eagle by providing cookies for our Family Day. Your efforts substantially improved the morale of our Soldiers and families alike. Soldier's Angels' help is in keeping with the highest tradition of support of the United States Army and Army Reserve.

15 July 2006

Michael G. Corrigan
MG, USAR
Commanding

Certificates and Awards

May No Soldier Go Unloved

Certificates and Awards

Several flags have been flown in Soldiers Angels' honor. The top certificate is about a flag which was flown in the U.S. Capitol by California Congressman Schiff, the lower flag was in combat in Iraq.

COMANCHE COMPANY
2nd Battalion 7th Cavalry Regiment

CERTIFICATE OF APPRECIATION

IS PRESENTED TO:

SOLDIER'S ANGELS

FOR THE SUPPORT YOU HAVE PROVIDED TO KEEP THESE MOUNTED
WARRIORS ON TOP OF THEIR GAME. YOU KEEP FOCUSED THE
FINEST ARMORED CREWMEN THE COUNTRY HAS TO OFFER TO
PLACE VIOLENCE AND SPEED DOWN ON THE ENEMIES OF OUR
GREAT LAND. THANK YOU FOR YOUR UNWAIVERING DEDICATION
DURING OPERATION IRAQI FREEDOM 06-08.
COMANCHES!!!

LIGHT 'EM UP!!

274

Certificates and Awards

May No Soldier Go Unloved

Award from Los Angeles County Board of Supervisors

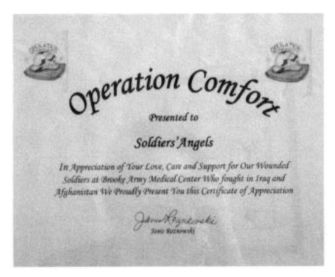

Certificates and Awards

The George Washington Spirit Award presented to Patti Patton Bader for Soldiers Angels contribution to the combat wounded. This is the highest award given by the Military Order of Purple Hearts to a non-member.

May No Soldier Go Unloved

Department of the Army Civilian Award for Humanitarian Service presented to Patti Patton Bader for Soldiers Angels Contribution to the combat wounded. This is the highest award that can be given to a Civilian by the Defense Department.

Certificates and Awards

Thank you for your support!! Your care package has really helped to boost our morale.

Sincerely, The Men and Women of KINGPIN

Certificate of Thanks

Presented this day, 15 December 2006, to

THE SOLDIERS ANGELS
Patti Patton-Bader

For supporting our Deployed Troops

Joint Area Support Group-Central (P)
International Zone (IZ)
US Embassy-Baghdad

SFC Charles A. Hiden
United States Army Chaplain Corp

Operation Iraqi Freedom (OIF)

May No Soldier Go Unloved

Guardian Angels For Soldier's Pet

CERTIFICATE OF APPRECIATION

This certificate of appreciation is gratefully presented to

Patti Patton-Bader - Soldiers' Angels

In recognition and sincere appreciation of outstanding service and assistance to the advancement of Guardian Angels For Soldier's Pet Program and Mission this Nineteenth day of September, 2005

Jim Olmedo, President

Carole Olmedo, Co-Founder

Linda Spurlin-Dominik, Co-Founder

TASK FORCE 399TH
OPERATION IRAQI FREEDOM
Certificate of Appreciation
is awarded to
Soldiers' Angels

399th COMBAT SUPPORT HOSPITAL

For outstanding contributions to the moral and welfare of the soldiers. Your efforts to lift the sprits and bring smiles to those soldiers in need of one. Your efforts greatly effected the overall success of our mission. The soldiers of the 399th Combat Support Hospital salute Soldiers' Angels.

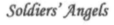

William Valliere
CSM, USA
MOSUL, IRAQ

Bryan R. Kelly
COL, USA
Commanding

Certificates and Awards

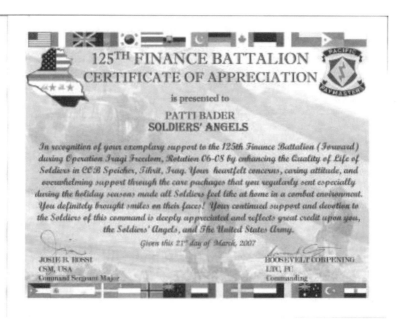

42d DISCOM

Certificate of Appreciation

is awarded to

Soldiers Angel

For outstanding contributions to the Morale and Professionalism of the 42nd Infantry Division. We would like to thank you for your letters, cards and gift boxes that made all the difference in our lives here in Iraq. Thank you for recognizing us, reaching out to us and taking the time to prepare those wonderful gifts.

Task Force Liberty – Operation Iraqi Freedom III
Awarded September 2005

DISCOM CSM

DISCOM Commander

148th Support Battalion
48th Brigade Combat Team

CERTIFICATE OF APPRECIATION

AWARDED TO

SOLDIER'S ANGELS

FOR YOUR SUPPORT OF THE MEN AND WOMEN OF THE GEORGIA ARMY NATIONAL GUARD. WE WOULD LIKE TO TAKE THIS OPPORTUNITY TO SAY THANK YOU FOR YOUR CARING CONTRIBUTION OF GIFTS TO THE SOLDIERS. YOU WILL ALWAYS BE TRULY APPRECIATED BY THE 148TH SUPPORT BATTALION DURING OPERATION IRAQI FREEDOM III.

GIVEN THIS 19th DAY OF APRIL, 2006
AT CAMP ADDER, TALLIL AB, IRAQ

CSM, USA
Command Sergeant Major

JEFFERY R. EDGE
LTC, QM
Commanding

Certificates and Awards

**2ND BATTALION,
227TH AVIATION REGIMENT
1ST CAVALRY DIVISION**

CERTIFICATE OF APPRECIATION
to
Soldiers' Angels

2-227TH Aviation Regiment, "LOBOS," thanks you for the sacrifices you made to purchase, pack and send our soldiers coffee mugs during Operation Iraqi Freedom 06-08. Your support is valued by the soldiers who appreciate the mugs and the command and staff who appreciate the care and concern you evidence by your sacrifice.

CHRISTOPHER A. JOSLIN
Lieutenant Colonel, U.S. Army
Commanding

1st Cavalry Division

3rd BRIGADE SPECIAL TROOPS BATTALION

CERTIFICATE OF APPRECIATION

IS PRESENTED TO

Soldier's Angels

Thank you for the generous gifts that your organization contributed to the Soldiers of the 3rd Brigade Special Troops Battalion during their deployment to Diyala Province, Iraq in support of Operation Iraqi Freedom. Your heartfelt donations were greatly appreciated and significantly contributed to raising the morale of our Soldiers during this Holiday season.

Thank You again for your support.

"Steadfast and Vigilant"

ARTHUR T. SWINGLER
Command Sergeant Major, USA

MICHAEL W. ROSE
Lieutenant Colonel, USA

291

Combined Joint Task Force - 76

Certificate of Appreciation

is hereby awarded to

Soldiers Angels

Thank you for your generous donations and support to the humanitarian mission to the people of Afghanistan. Your generosity has touched many lives!

Major Catherine Bradshaw
Catherine Bradshaw, PA
CJTF Humanitarian Civic Assistance
CJTF-76 CJ4

January 1, 2007

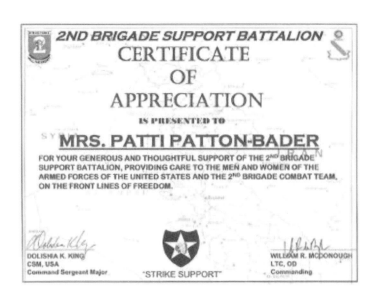

2ND BRIGADE SUPPORT BATTALION

CERTIFICATE OF APPRECIATION

IS PRESENTED TO

MRS. PATTI PATTON-BADER

FOR YOUR GENEROUS AND THOUGHTFUL SUPPORT OF THE 2ND BRIGADE SUPPORT BATTALION, PROVIDING CARE TO THE MEN AND WOMEN OF THE ARMED FORCES OF THE UNITED STATES AND THE 2ND BRIGADE COMBAT TEAM, ON THE FRONT LINES OF FREEDOM.

DOLISHIA K. KING
CSM, USA
Command Sergeant Major

"STRIKE SUPPORT"

WILLIAM R. MCDONOUGH
LTC, OD
Commanding

Certificates and Awards

May No Soldier Go Unloved

Patti receiving the George Washington Spirit Award on behalf of Soldiers Angels at the annual convention of the Military Order of the Purple Hearts (Los Angeles, CA. 2006)

Patti accepting the Civilian Humanitarian Award (Pasadena, CA. 2006)
Her Angel pin seems to have a halo

14

Living Legend Trees

"Military history is replete with time honored traditions. None are more sacred than those which honor our country's military dead. The military code of "leave no man behind" insures a soldier that his sacrifice will be honored from the moment he dies on the battlefield that his remains will be treated with the dignity and respect accorded a brother in arms. In every conflict there are examples of soldiers honoring these traditions, sometimes with their own lives. One can not fathom the enormity of emotions running through the family and friends of these brave soldiers. We can only hope when these horrifying times become history pages that it was all for something. That

Living Legend Trees

the world is a more peaceful place and the deaths of our soldiers is seen as nothing less than a heroic sacrifice. To die in a strange land with hatred and viciousness makes our battle all the more daunting and hard to stay the course. If we break now, it will be as though it would have been for naught. We reach out to the loved ones of the slain and with hope and faith we hold them in our hearts forever." - Patti Patton Bader

Sometimes Patti is so close to war and both the tragedies and emotions that accompany it, that I thank my lucky stars I can *escape to my job* and worry about the more mundane things like putting food on the table and keeping a roof over our heads. After a year of making memorial pages for our fallen heroes and comforting mothers, fathers, sisters, brothers, wives and husbands of those killed in action, Patti formed the Living Legends Team in April 2004.

Soldiers Angels Living Legends Team members are people of extreme dedication and have sworn to be on the Living Legends Team for each and every one of their lifetimes. Not everyone is suited to be on the Living Legends Team. This team of Angels provides aid and assistance to the families of heroes who have perished protecting our freedoms and way of life. These team members attend the funerals of the fallen and call their families yearly on those anniversaries to remind them we have not forgotten the sacrifices of their loved ones.

Soldiers Angels provides a "Living Tree" to the family of each fallen hero. It is Soldiers Angels vision that these trees will grow and flourish so all remember these fallen heroes bravery and heroism. Living Trees have been proudly planted at parks, schools and city halls.

The program started with Brian H., the father of a fallen hero. Brian H.'s son died heroically while patrolling the streets of Kirkut, Iraq in an unarmored vehicle when he and his unit were ambushed. Brian's son, John, fought back ferociously, but while he was reloading his gun, he was mortally wounded when enemy bullets ripped through the unarmored vehicle he was taking cover against - instantly killing him.

It was Mr. H.'s belief that his son might have survived if he had been protected in an armored vehicle. "When he died, all his ammunition had been spent," the unit commander wrote in a letter to H's parents. "Your son gave everything he had for the safety of others.... As a commander, I struggle to find words that adequately capture the depth to which we honor Private First Class John H." Mr. H contacted Patti when he found a tribute she had written about John in her daily blog on the Iraq War.

Mr. H. conveyed his concern about the unarmored vehicles the troops were using. Patti encouraged Mr. H. to "do something about it," and he did. Mr H. wrote to congressmen and women, senators, called newspaper, radio, and T.V. stations and blogged daily about the lack of body armor and armored vehicles in Iraq. Working the Internet and phones daily, Mr. H learned about additional soldiers who had been killed in unarmored Humvees. He became an outspoken critic, appearing on national radio shows, granting newspaper interviews and making trips to meet with politicians in Washington, D.C. Turning grief into action, his efforts paid off. The military began to provide more body armor for our soldiers and re-armor their vehicles, especially the dangerous Humvees that most troops were using for patrols.

A year later, Mr H. received a letter from a mother whose son had lost a foot in an IED attack in Baghdad. She wanted to thank him for saving her son's life. The vehicle her son had been riding in had recently been re-armored. Mr. H. sent the mother's letter to Patti, telling her that it was Patti's motivation and support that was partially responsible for such a humbling letter and wonderful feeling of accomplishment. He had saved at least one life! (God Bless You Mr. H., you have saved thousands of lives!)

Patti wanted to do something special to honor Mr. H's son, John. She wanted something which would not be forgotten - something beautiful which would grow to be strong - like John. Patti told Mr. H that she would like to plant a "Living Legends Tree" for John. The tree was planted with a plaque honoring John's service during a Memorial Day celebration at the local park in John's hometown. Mr. and Mrs. H. sometimes drive out of their way to go visit John's tree and wrote to Patti, thanking her for the idea of the Living Legends Tree. Mr. H requested another Living Legends Tree and plaque for his neighbor, a marine's father, who had also recently lost his son in battle in Al Fallujah, Iraq. The Living Legend Tree program had been born. Since then, Soldiers Angels has provided Living Legend Trees to numerous families of the fallen and it is Soldiers Angels ambition to provide a Living Legend Tree to the families of every fallen hero.

Cathy W., the team leader of the Living Legends project says, "The team has tried to express the sorrow and grief that we know all Americans feel for the loss of our precious and beloved soldiers. So many have sacrificed for our freedoms; we hope this helps to ensure that we never forget what it takes to keep our liberties."

"Patti,

I just wanted to let you know that the two trees sent to us in Bed-ford, MA survived the winter. The little dogwoods for John H (airborne) and Travis D (marines) killed in our town are planted at the entrance of the Memorial Park. There will be a Memorial

May No Soldier Go Unloved

Day ceremony where a name stone is dedicated for Travis who was killed in November in Falloujah. It will go next to John's who was killed in Oct. 03 near Kirkuk. I promised you a picture and will send it as soon as the flowers bloom over there. Anyway, the H's and the D's wanted to thank you and yours for this fine thought."

Cathy

Dear Cathy,

Thank you for the beautiful Pygmy Date Palm its really nice. I got it yesterday. Please thank everyone that made this possible. It will always remind us of Joe. I will be place it at his favorite placed in my parents house, a back room where he would love to play his drums.

The C. Family

Living Legend Trees

Dear Cathy,

We would like to thank you and the Living Legends for the "But-terfly" magnolia tree you gave us in memory of our son, Stephen. We are looking forward to its blossoms in the spring. Although Stephen was fulfilling what he believed was his calling, the loss has been great. We truly appreciate what Living Legends is doing to honor fallen heroes. Thank you for your prayers and cards of sympathy. May God bless you.

Sincerely,

Bill and Sue F.

May No Soldier Go Unloved

Dear Soldiers Angels,

One day my daughter, PFC Amy D., excitedly called me from Iraq and told me she had several Soldiers Angels. I smiled and thanked God for people who would care for and pray for my daughter; people we don't even know. It blessed my heart and those of my family very much. For reasons that only God and Savior knows, Amy went to be with our Lord on March 11th after dying from a gunshot wound that she received on March 8th. The reason that I am writing is to thank you and tell you how much I appreciated your ministry to my daughter and to my whole family. The cards, letters, and gifts comforted and blessed us. Your compassion and love for soldiers and their families has reached people you will never know about until you are with our Lord too. Thank you and may our Lord richly bless you and your ministry.

Sustained in Him,

Chaplain (Major) Doug and Michelle D., Baltimore, MD.

Living Legend Trees

Patti Bader and Soldiers Angels,

Tell everyone thank-you for all the cards they have sent to us. It helps getting cards knowing that there are people out there that haven't forgotten Justin. Thank-You so much. The hand stamp is neat and pretty. Thanks. We can not forget any of the soldiers that didn't make it home. (KIA's) We think about all them still over there fighting and risking their lives.

Thanks.

Sincerely,

Bill and Robin H. parents of SPC. Justin W. H. 8-1-03

May No Soldier Go Unloved

Cathy,

Thank You for the wonderful letter. Even after the death of my husband, you still continue to care for him. My husband looked forward to hearing from each and every Soldiers Angel. They brought great joy in his lonely times. He was a wonderful husband, father, and soldier. He truly loved the Army and his soldiers. I will never forget you or any other Soldiers Angel. Thank you for keeping all of our soldiers in your thoughts and prayers. You are truly a blessing! "The true measure of a man is how he treats someone who can do him absolutely no good." – Samuel Johnson 1709-1784

God bless,

Stephenie, Cameron, and Bayleigh D.

Living Legend Trees

Dear Friends,

How can I possibly tell you how much we appreciate all the cards, flowers, and phone calls we have received from so many of you. Your prayers and support are getting us through a very tough time in our lives. We love you all! Thank you, too, for the donations made to our son, Trevor's memorial fund. We are hoping to use the money to buy "Mist N Go Vests" for the Army unit Trevor belonged to in Iraq. The vests are designed to keep the troops cool in the desert heat. You can see them on line under Body Armor. In this way we can serve our troops as they continue to fight for our freedom. Again we thank each one of you for all your support.

Rick and Debi W.

Blessed is the nation whose God is the Lord Psalm 33:12

May No Soldier Go Unloved

Dear Soldiers Angels,

Thank you for your generous donation to our son's memorial fund. Cynthia N. forwarded is on to us. We truly appreciate your precious letter. God bless you for all you do.

Dear friend,

I am sending this letter to thank you for supporting my son and the troops while they were/are serving in Iraq. My son, David U., kept every letter and envelope sent to him, I know this because his family and I received them back on November 8th, 2006 with the rest of his personal items. You see, these meant a lot to David so he saved them. They continue to mean a lot to us also as David was killed October 17th 2006 by an I.E.D. in Iraq he would of turned 22 on Oct 31. Your kind letters and drawings are helping us through this huge loss. We are proud to see he was supported by all of you while there. Now let me tell you about the soldier/young man whose heart you touched. David was born, David Michael U. on October 31, 1984 at 4:08 a.m. He weighed 6 pds 7 ½ oz. and was 16 ¾ inches long. David

Living Legend Trees

*grew up in Leavenworth Kansas. He is the oldest of five chil-
dren. He has two brothers, Jeremy, age 18, and Shane, age 12
and two sisters, Joni, age 13 and Sadie age 3. He loved his little
brothers and sisters very much and was a wonderful role model,
protector, and friend to all of them. David graduated high
school May 23, 2003. On August 21st, 2003, he left for basic
training (Ft. Knox, Kentucky) His specialty (MOS) was a 19 Kilo
(tanker). He married his wife, Laura, on February 14th 2004.
They gave us a beautiful grandson, Gage, on February 7th, 2005.
David loved his wife and son. He couldn't wait to come home to
Gage so he could be the father he couldn't be for over a year in
Iraq. He loved horseback riding, dogs, cats, video/computer
games, and dancing. David could bring a smile (he did this quite
often) to even a mother getting ready to hand down punishment
for something done wrong! David worked at the Main Post
Chapel on Ft. Leavenworth until 2 days before leaving for basic
training. He touched many lives from the time he was 13 until he
left for basic. He had a HUGE heart! David had an air about
him that could put you at total ease and make you smile or laugh*

anytime. He was our comic relief as was also to his fellow sol-diers in Iraq. At his funeral he had in excess of 2,000 people in attendance. Military, civilians, teachers, friends, family and complete strangers turned out to pay their respects to this won-derful young man who I am proud to call my son. I felt the need to write to every one that sent a letter. I don't know if David had time to write you back but please know you did touch his life. I am thanking you for taking the time to send that letter or picture. I will put them very carefully into a scrap book for his son to read and look at some day.

Much love and appreciation,

Diana P. Proud mother of Cpl. David U.

15

Hurricane Katrina - Above and Beyond

In August 2005, The Louisiana National Guard finished their
year tour in Iraq. Hurricane Katrina had struck two weeks earlier
and the Army made special provisions for them when they returned "home". The Army gave these soldiers 48 hours of
special leave to find their love ones, briefly take care of their affairs and secure any property and possessions. The members of
the Guard would then have to immediately report back to their
units for further orders.

Normally, the Army would keep those soldiers returning
from combat duty on base for a couple of weeks to "decom-
press" them and slowly assimilate them back into civilian life

before they allowed them to go home and visit their loved ones. Usually, the Army checked soldiers for signs of Post Traumatic Stress Disorder (PTSD). The Army didn't want any of their servicemen committing road rage when cut off by little old ladies from Pasadena.

Because the New Orleans Airport was not operational, the Army flew the returning Guard members to the nearest airport in Alexandria, LA. It was then up to the soldiers to locate their families to get them home. There was a significant problem with that plan though. Anyone who had been living in New Orleans or the Gulf Coast didn't *have* a home anymore and more importantly, their families were refugees in other cities around the country. An attorney from Shreveport, LA, Ricky J., who had worked with Patti previously by donating his airline miles, called Patti to tell her of the Louisiana National Guard's plight. Ricky J. and Patti started working together to create a fund for the returning soldiers.

Patti made contact with the Louisiana National Guard Rear Detachment Liaisons. As the Guardsman landed, they lined up at

312

two special phones, told Patti and I where they needed to go and Patti and I frantically booked their flights via Expedia's website. After we had maxed out the limit on the corporation credit cards, we started maxing out our own. The first plane landed around 3:30 A.M. our time and by 3 P.M. in the afternoon we had booked flights for all the Guard members who needed a flight - except for six unlucky guys who were trying to get to a few of the smaller and less populous locations. Alexandria has a small airport and there are not many flights going in and out. The airport is so small that it actually shuts down at night. Patti and I booked roundtrip flights to everywhere imaginable: Miami, Houston, Los Angeles, Dallas, Little Rock, Louisville, city by city the list goes on and on; but it looked like we wouldn't be able to get the remaining six servicemen out of Alexandria until the next day.

Patti arranged for free rooms for the soldiers from hotels and coordinated with gracious businessmen who donated a dinner to each soldier. But, even with all of the generosity, it didn't seem fair that after all these servicemen had been through, they would be stuck in Alexandria - like an old Bob Dylan song. This would

only give them 24 hours leave before they had to report back to

duty and probably be instantly deployed to cleaning up Katrina's

mess. Adding insult to injury, some of these servicemen didn't

even know *where* their family members actually were. I can't

even imagine the overwhelming stress laid on these six soldiers

and the general feeling of panic and ungratefulness that must

have overcome them. We could hear the desperation, anxiety

and helplessness in their voices.

For hours we tried to no avail to get these guys "home" to

their families. Time was running out. Soon, the airport was go-

ing to shut down until the next morning. Most of the stranded six

soldiers had already resolved themselves to spending the night in

Alexandria. At the last minute, when we finally knew for certain

we couldn't get them out, Patti made some quick phone calls and

hired a private jet in Houston to pick them up at the Alexandria

Airport. From there, they would be air taxied to the airports

closest to their displaced families.

The jet barely made it out before the airport closed, but every member of the Louisiana National Guard made it home to their family that night via Soldiers Angels. The jet flew them individually to Austin and San Antonio, TX, Memphis, TN, Rome, GA, Charleston, SC and Ft. Lauderdale, FL. The "stuck six" called us from the pilot's cell phone as the jet took off from Alexandria. On the phone Patti and I could hear six very happy soldiers and one real cool pilot chanting as loud as they could, "ANGELS, ANGELS, ANGELS, ANGELS, ANGELS, ANGELS, ANGELS, ANGELS, ANGELS, ANGELS!"

May No Soldier Go Unloved

Dear Patti,

My son was stationed in Iraq with the 256th out of New Orleans in 2004-2005, returning only 2 weeks after Katrina destroyed our home. We were in Ft. Lauderdale, FL staying with relatives when my son returned home & I didn't have a car to drive back to Louisiana to get him. Your organization chartered a flight for him & 5 other soldiers to reunite them with their displaced families. Thank you, Thank you, Thank you, for bringing my son to me when I was unable to get to him on my own. My gift may not be much, $100.00 but it is sent with enormous gratitude & hope that it can be used to make another soldier's life a little happier, a little better. God bless you & your organization!

Sincerely,

Gwen K. C., MS Hello,

Hurricane Katrina - Above and beyond

Dear Mrs. Patti,

You are a true Angel. I wish I could express in words how I feel in my heart. I would like to thank you very much for the check to help me bear with the expenses of the hurricane. The money will be very helpful since I have no income for three weeks. I was not able to get to my home to evaluate the damage until around 1 ½ weeks ago. It is unbelievable what Mother Nature can deal you, but with everyone's prayers this too shall pass. It has been an emotional roller coaster but will get better. The money you sent me will come to well use. You are a wonderful organization and a caring organization. It was difficult for my son to be in Iraq and worrying about me. I am a heart patient and am legally blind in one eye and I am his only parent alive. His Angel Jen has been wonderful to both of us. I have adopted her as a daughter. She is a lovely person. Even though we have never met I feel as though I have known her for years. Thank you for all that your organization does for the soldiers. I know my son he always said he felt like he had a lot of the love he had at home. He al-

May No Soldier Go Unloved

ways would say – Mom people really do care about us.

Once again thank you and may God Bless You.

Slena H and Spc.Thomas L., Beaumont, TX

I work in the Army Well-Being Liaison Office. Last year during our Hurricane Katrina response, Patti Bader and Soldier's Angels were phenomenal. Ms. Bader called our office and asked what could she do to help. Her care and concern for our Soldiers and family members is deeply appreciated. I would like to receive the instructions to make the Blankets of Hope.

Thank you for all you do for our Soldiers.

Cathy D. J. Special Projects Officer Office of the Deputy Chief of Staff, G-1 Army Well-Being Liaison Office

16

My Favorite Angel Moment

There have been so many compelling Soldiers Angels moments that I will always remember. I can close my eyes and still see some of those moments clearly now as if they were happening all over again.

Standing and reciting the Pledge of Allegiance and singing the National Anthem with the Veterans at the convention of the Military Order of Purple Hearts in Los Angeles.

While we were visiting Scotts Air Force Base, the heartwarming tears of thanks we received from a mother who's son was wounded in combat and had received a first response backpack from Soldiers Angels.

May No Soldier Go Unloved

Meeting the staff and families of wounded heroes while visiting several Fisher Houses around the country. Visiting with the wounded and staff at Brook Army Medical Center (BAMC) in San Antonio and the Walter Reed Medical Facility in Washington D.C.

Taking a private tour of the National Medical Naval Center at Bethesda with SSGT S and visiting a wounded hero who was wearing a Soldiers Angels sweatshirt and pants he had received 10 days earlier at Bagram Medical Center Iraq and had been wearing it since.(Amazingly Soldiers Angels had just produced and shipped the clothes less than 3 weeks earlier).

Seeing the amputee soldiers riding their special bikes and wheelchairs down to the ocean during operation "Soldier Ride," as the band played the song "We Are the Champions" to them and the thousands who had gathered.

That day Americans lined the streets of San Clemente, CA to cheer these wounded soldiers on while proudly waving American flags. These brave Iraqi War amputees rode special bicycles and wheelchairs across the country, from the Atlantic to

My Favorite Angel Moment

the Pacific, to raise awareness and funds for a recreational center they wanted built for other amputees and wounded soldiers.

I'll never forget the sight of a proud Army wife on San Clemente beach picking up her double amputee husband off his stuck wheelchair in the sand, proudly kissing him and carrying him the last few feet into the Pacific Ocean.

The memory of those wounded heroes celebrating in the water as the crowd cheered "USA, USA, USA," still makes the hair on my arms stand up and my eyes to swell proudly with tears. I can still see the sunset over the ocean from that night, smell the BBQ and hear the hero's laughing.

Soldiers Angels was providing hotel rooms, food and entertainment for these "soldier riders" on the last leg of their journey and I followed their progress for weeks by going to the soldier ride website. When the riders got to the Colorado River, Patti and I donated funds for a couple of hours of jet skiing for all the guys.

Like most Soldiers Angels adoptions, the people I have written, helped or bought things for, I have and never would meet.

May No Soldier Go Unloved

Seeing these handicapped heroes in person and seeing their appreciation of what Soldiers Angels was doing for them and the sincere way they *thanked me* that day – when I felt as though I should be the one *thanking them* for their courage and sacrifices was one of the most humbling and emotional experiences of my life and one I will never forget and cherish forever.

My favorite Soldiers Angels moment comes accompanied with a Rod Serling soundtrack and always gives me goose bumps when I tell it. It is the tale of an unfortunate corporal who was seriously wounded by an IED while riding in an unarmored Humvee on combat patrol in Iraq. He tragically lost part of his face, a leg and an arm in the explosion and went into a uninduced coma. He was stabilized in Iraq and immediately flown to the Army Hospital in Landstuhl, Germany. He was scheduled to fly to Walter Reed Army Medical Hospital in Washington D.C. for numerous complicated face surgeries in the next few days.

Because he was adopted by an Angel, Patti became aware of his situation and contacted his mother to see if there was anything Soldiers Angels could do to help. Patti informed her that

My Favorite Angel Moment

she had Angels in Germany that were available to help or deliver anything needed. The mother asked if one of the Angels would go to Landstuhl Regional Medical Center and sit with her son and hold a cell phone to his ear while she talked to him from Utah. She would be flying to Washington D.C. the next day to be with her son upon his arrival to Walter Reed. Patti asked an Angel living near Landstuhl if she could help. At the arranged time, the mother called and the Angel held the cell phone to the Corporal's one good ear and held on to his one good hand. He had been in a coma for over 72 hours. At the sound of his mother's voice, the soldier squeezed the Angels hand and within a few hours came out of his coma.

17

May No Soldier Go Unloved

Soldiers Angels mission is to aid and support deployed soldiers and their families. Soldiers Angels started out sending care packages and letters, but as Patti became aware of more situations that needed support, Soldiers Angels grew and morphed into teams that were incorporated to handle specific needs. Soldiers Angels now has a board of directors, president, vice president, secretary and treasurer – in addition to the volunteers who head up 50 State Chapters and Special Work Teams. Soldiers Angels has grown internationally and now has an international president, and chapters in Germany, France, Poland, England, Australia, New Zealand and Canada. Soldiers Angels is 100 % volunteer run and 100% of all donations are spent directly on aiding the mission of Soldiers Angels. Not one officer or board member is paid or derives a salary from Soldiers

Angels. As Patti would say, "Soldiers Angels believes that little

ripples of kindness add up to oceans of greatness." Soldiers An-

gels is an organization made-up of generous Americans who

give their time, money, heart and souls, to support the brave men

and women of our military wherever we raise our flag. "The

heart of a volunteer is immeasurable."

Patti likes to tell people how they can help. "If you've got

some money, write a check, if you don't have a lot of money,

write a letter." If you wish to make a financial donation to Sol-

diers Angels (or a specific team project) send a check or go to

http://www.soldiersangels.org and contribute by credit card or

PayPal. Soldiers Angels is a non-profit organization and our tax

number for your tax deduction is Tax ID # 20-0583415. If you

wish to adopt a soldier and become a Soldiers Angel, simply go

to the website http://www.soldiersangels.org and sign up. We

ask Soldiers Angels to send a card or a letter a week and at least

one care package a month to your "adoptee." It is Patti's and

Soldiers Angels' belief that soldiers who are adopted have a better chance to come home "healthy" and have less stress and have

a better chance of not having Post Traumatic Stress Disorder.

You don't need to adopt a soldier or make a financial donation

to help.

Here are some of Soldiers Angels volunteer teams you can

join that require no monetary contributions. The Letter Writing

Team is one of our most successful teams. The Angels on this

team receive a new soldier's name each week and pen letters of

encouragement and support to our deployed soldiers. The Card

and Letters Team is comprised of Angels at the ready - to send

holiday and special occasion cards. This year, the Angels sent a

December holiday package and a letter of thanks to every service

member stationed in Iraq and Afghanistan. Soldiers Angels also

has Angels on the Wounded Team. These Angels visit the com-

bat hospitals to support the wounded heroes and their families.

The Angels Veterans Team visits local veteran hospitals. Volun-

teer Angels sew Blankets of Hope for our First Response

Backpacks. Operation Top Knot helps the babies of our heroes

and Operation Outreach helps the families of the deployed. The

May No Soldier Go Unloved

Living Legends Team helps the families of the fallen and the Welcome Home team helps provide greetings by providing supplies and welcoming our returning heroes back to the States.

It's not that Patti Patton Bader is moving mountains, but rather she is showing us that collectively mountains can truly be moved. Volunteerism is a natural human endeavor and Soldiers Angels is one of those noble causes that naturally resonates within all of us patriotic Americans. Very few of us have the ability to change history but each of us has a chance to change a small portion of the events by contributing a little of our time or money. Together, all combined, these numerous acts of generosity can and will shape the future of this great country. Supporting those who put their life on the line to protect our precious freedom doesn't get any simpler then Patti's Soldiers Angels motto: May no soldier go unloved. May no soldier walk alone. May no soldier be forgotton. Until they all come home.

May No Soldier Go Unloved

Jeff and Patti Patton Bader live in sleepy Pasadena, California with their five long haired Chihuahua's; Jerry, Scarlet, Madison, Oscar, and Angel. They have three children: Bayley, Brandon, and Brett.

Jeff founded and manages the corporation Accurate Credit Bureau from his offices downstairs which conveniently has a residential home upstairs where Jeff, Patti, and the herd reside. Jeff played with the rock band Rifficus Rose for many years and continues to write and record original music. You can read more about Jeff and Patti, and/or purchase his music or this book by going to the website www.jeffbader.com.